D0129105

LOWELL LIBSON LTD · 2014

NEW YORK: JANUARY 25 – FEBRUARY 1
Annual exhibition at Mitchell-Innes & Nash:
British Art: Recent Acquisitions
& *Thomas Gainsborough: The Landscape of Refinement*

LONDON: FEBRUARY 17 – FEBRUARY 28
Thomas Gainsborough: The Landscape of Refinement

MAASTRICHT: MARCH 14 – 23
TEFAF: The European Fine Art Fair

LONDON: JULY 4 – JULY 11
Master Drawings & Sculpture Week
London Art Week

LONDON: OCTOBER 16 – OCTOBER 19
Frieze Masters

LOWELL LIBSON LTD

2014

LOWELL LIBSON LTD

3 Clifford Street · London W1S 2LF
Telephone: +44 (0)20 7734 8686
Fax: +44 (0)20 7734 9997
Email: pictures@lowell-libson.com
Website: www.lowell-libson.com

The gallery is open by appointment, Monday to Friday
The entrance is in Old Burlington Street

Lowell Libson
lowell@lowell-libson.com

Deborah Greenhalgh
deborah@lowell-libson.com

Jonny Yarker
jonny@lowell-libson.com

Published by Lowell Libson Limited 2014
Text and publication © Lowell Libson Limited
All rights reserved

ISBN 978 0 9563930 7 4

Cover: a sheet of 18th-century Italian
paste paper (collection: Lowell Libson)

Frontispiece: Francis Cotes RA 1726–1770
Detail from *Mary Colebrooke, later Lady Aubrey*, 1766

Photography by Rodney Todd White & Son Ltd
Designed and typeset in Dante by Dalrymple
Colour reproduction by Altaimage
Printed in Belgium by Albe De Coker

CONTENTS

OUR ANNUAL CATALOGUE RELIES ENTIRELY ON THE WORKS WE HAVE IN HAND
and it is this serendipity that gives each of these volumes an individual character.
We hope, nonetheless, that our offering for 2014 demonstrates a consistency in the
quality and the interest of the works of art that we delight in handling.

This year the catalogue seems to have three distinct groupings: a selection of
paintings, drawings and sculpture made in or inspired by Italy. This includes the
most fascinating ruinscape by Arthur Devis, an extremely powerful and important drawing by Joseph Wright of Derby, beautiful watercolours by J.R. Cozens
and Flaxman's exceptional carving of the *Adoration of the Magi*, a masterpiece of
European neo-classicism.

A group of portraits, including: Francis Cotes's wonderful pastel of Mary
Colebrooke in its equally marvellous frame; representative examples of pastels
by Daniel Gardner and Hugh Douglas Hamilton. Charles James Fox, the giant
of late eighteenth-century politics is depicted in Hamilton's pastel made for the
sitter's cousin, the 2nd Duke of Leinster, as well as by Thomas Lawrence, in what
is possibly the most psychologically engaging of all the portraits of this larger
than life figure. Lawrence's early masterpiece of 1791, his study of Arthur Atherley,
demonstrates all the qualities that was to make this future President of the Royal
Academy the most renowned portraitist in Europe.

Another theme is 'on the spot' landscape studies. The sequence of Turner
sketchbook pages of 1824 show this great artist at his most incisive and they
demonstrate the various techniques that he was able to employ with such prowess
whilst working *en plein air*. This is a quality demonstrated in Edward Lear's great
drawing of the Cedars of Lebanon executed twenty years later, in a watercolour
study which he considered one of his masterpieces.

This year this catalogue is accompanied by a second volume devoted to the
work of Thomas Gainsborough.

I am extremely grateful to Jonny Yarker who has researched and written many
of the entries in this catalogue and to Deborah Greenhalgh who, as always, has
dealt with all other details of its production with her usual efficiency.

LOWELL LIBSON

Victor-Marie Hugo 1802–1885, *Landscape*
Detail at seven times magnification of pen and ink drawing
1½ × 4⅜ inches · 38 × 112 mm

WILLIAM JOHN BANKES 1786–1855

Two Wings of an Altarpiece

Watercolour and gouache on vellum
22¼ × 7½ inches · 565 × 188 mm
Painted *circa* 1804.

COLLECTIONS
William John Bankes, Trinity College,
Cambridge *c.*1804;
Private collection, 2013.

George Sanders (1774–1846)
William James Bankes, 1812
Kingston Lacy, Dorset
© National Trust / Derrick E. Witty

This remarkable pair of panels were made by the great connoisseur and collector William Bankes to decorate the Gothic 'chapel' he created in his set of rooms at Trinity College, Cambridge, in 1803. The 'chapel', elements of which still survive in the south range of Trinity's Great Court, was the whimsical creation of Bankes, the richest and most exuberant of a remarkable group of undergraduates, which included George Gordon, Lord Byron. Bankes would go on to become one of the greatest art collectors of the first quarter of the nineteenth century, but more than this, he proved himself to be one of the most innovative decorators of the period, creating a series of unprecedented interiors at his Dorset house, Kingston Lacy. These panels, along with the surviving interior of the 'chapel' itself, give a remarkable early insight into his artistic inventiveness and tastes.

In a letter to his grandmother, Bankes explained the disposition of his rooms at Trinity shortly after matriculating in November 1803, noting he had a large drawing room:

about the size of one of the front rooms in Palace Yard [the Bankes's London home]. It is uncommonly neatly, though not expensively, furnished, and my bedroom is very suitable to it with all its accoutrements. I have also a third room which has no fireplace and I use it rather as a light closet than a dwelling room. Three of my windows look into the quadrangle and one looks backward with a view of Caius College, Trinity Hall and King's Chapel … My library is a very great and useful ornament to my rooms, which are now as well furnished as any in college.[1]

It was in the 'light closet' which Bankes created a remarkable essay in early neo-Gothic design, inserting a theatrically

molded Gothic ceiling painted with armorial escutcheons, the vaulting supported by angel-headed bosses, on the walls he had painted a screen of Gothic decoration and the plain seventeenth-century College windows fronted with faux-Gothic tracery. The furniture of this small room – which Bankes himself christened the 'Chapel' – also included an altar.

It is clear that the interior achieved a degree of celebrity during Bankes's residence in College. Writing in 1822, the year Bankes had been elected MP for Cambridge University, the great Trinity scientist Adam Sedgwick noted: 'Our representative Bankes is certainly a very extraordinary man, and possesses a wonderful fund of entertaining anecdotes. When an undergraduate he was half suspected of being a Papist: and he almost frightened Dr Ramsden to death, by building in his rooms an altar at which he daily burned incense, and frequently had the singing-boys dressed in their surplices to chant services.'[2] According to Byron, Bankes was fond of '*profane* jests' and this certainly seems to explain the spirit of Bankes's rooms: the false ceiling, painted decoration, incense and choir boys in costume. It was an interior designed in full sympathy with those created by Horace Walpole at Strawberry Hill and – perhaps more potently – William Beckford at Fonthill, which was close to the Bankes's estate, Kingston Lacy. Indeed Bankes's sense of the theatrical was legendary and much commented upon by contemporaries, the poet Thomas Moore noted that having: 'fitted up some of his rooms in imitation of a Catholic Chapel and used to have the Singing Boys in dress suitable to the occasion, come and sing there for him, and it was constantly asked "what

the devil does Mr Bankes do with those singing boys?'[3]

Bankes was a talented amateur artist and a large number of drawings from his Continental travels survive at Kingston Lacy, underlining his ability as a draughtsman and his intense interest in Gothic architecture. Bankes's spare, minutely observed studies of tracery and funerary monuments accord in style to the present panels. Surviving correspondence from Bankes's uncle, Sir William Wynne, reveals the antiquarian sources for his decoration. Wynne sent him prints of Durham and Exeter cathedrals, noting: 'I apprehend what you have already … will supply you with as many Gothick ornaments as can well be employed in the intended improvements of your rooms.'[4]

The iconography of these panels is completely in-tune with both Bankes's scholarly interest in architecture and his sense of humour. The left hand-panel comprises a kneeling knight, in a gilded tunic with the Bankes coat of arms – composed of four fleur-de-lis - hanging round his neck and behind him a bunch of lilies. Issuing from the figure's mouth is a Latin inscription – 'Domine Labia Mea Apenies' [Thou O Lord wilt open my lips] – taken from the first line of the Office of Matins. Above the kneeling figure, an angel holds a scroll containing the inscription: 'Gloria in excelsis Deo' [Glory to God in the Highest], and above this William Bankes's coat of arms, personalised with the addition of a crescent to denote his status as a second son. This helps in dating the panels, which must have been completed before the death of Bankes's brother, Henry, in 1806. The Bankes arms are entwined with the tendrils of a strawberry plant and rose, a strawberry appearing in the border at the bottom of the panel suggests it may also have had some heraldic or personal significance. The whole scene is set against a complex and dense design of Gothic tracery, probably copied from one of the engravings of Durham or Exeter cathedrals sent by Wynne.

Its pair, the right-hand panel, points to the mood and interpretation of the work. Designed to be correspondingly symmetrical, the kneeling figure has been replaced by a series of hooded, black-cloaked mourners holding tall candles with a pair of inscriptions reading: 'Orate pro anima Wulie' [Pray for the soul of Wulie]. They are arranged around a coffin, draped in a black pall, embroidered with the words: 'Vanitas Vanitatous Omnia Vanitas' [Vanity of Vanities all is Vanity]. Replacing the Bankes coat of arms, is a skull with the words – 'non deus est mourton' [God is not dead] – minutely inscribed in the mouth, and an exquisitely rendered fly perched on the dome of the skull. It is this combination of iconography which suggests that the panels represent the ultimate 'profane jest', acting as a monument to Bankes's own death. The hooded figures are clearly praying for the soul of William [Wulie] and following closely the conventions of medieval funerary iconography, the kneeling figure on the left-hand panel can be read as a self-portrait of Bankes himself. In the context of Bankes's role as the 'father of all mischief', as Byron called him, and the elaborate setting of the present panels in his rooms at university, they demand to be read as a joke, perhaps underscoring Bankes's obvious lack of virtues.[5]

The survival of a pair of these narrow panels begs the question of their original position and function within the 'Chapel' in Bankes's rooms at Trinity. One proposal has been that they formed part of an early English screen which belonged to Bankes and which is now on loan to St Edmundsbury Cathedral, Bury St Edmunds. The size, format and subject-matter of the present works do not quite match that of the fourteenth-century altarpiece from Bankes's collection, but the suggestion does raise the

Ceiling of Bankes's Gothic 'Chapel', Trinity College, Cambridge, showing the Bankes coat of arms prominently in the centre.

possibility that the panels were used to flank an existing work or another panel made by Bankes which has been subsequently lost. In their sophistication and playfulness they are an exceptional survival from Bankes's earliest known essay in interior decoration and are an important survival of early neo-Gothicism.

NOTES

1 Dorset History Centre, D/BKL, William John Bankes to Margaret Bankes, Cambridge, 1 November, 1803.

2 eds. J. Clark and T. Hughes, *The Life and Letters of Rev. Adam Sedwick*, Cambridge, 1890, I, p.259.

3 ed. W. S. Dowden, *Journal of Thomas Moore*, 1983–1991, IV, p.1540.

4 Dorset History Centre, D/BKL, William Wynn to William John Bankes, 12 November, 1804.

5 Ed. Rowland Prothero, *The Works of Lord Byron: Letters and Journals*, London, 1922, I, p.120.

JAMES BARRY RA 1741–1806

The Education of Achilles

Pen and brown ink over pencil on paper
13¾ × 10⅝ inches · 350 × 270 mm
Signed lower right: '*J Barry Inv.*', inscribed
verso: '*Phthengomia ois Themis estin thusan
epithestho Bebeloir / pasin omois – Orpheus –.*'
Stamped lower left with an unidentified
collectors mark: '*CHB*'
Drawn in 1772

COLLECTIONS

Alister Mathews;
Ralph Holland, acquired from the above,
June 1951;
By descent until 2013

James Barry travelled to Italy in 1766 with
the single aim, as he wrote to his friend and
patron Edmund Burke, of: 'forming myself
for a history painter.'[1] In practice this meant
studying the greatest sculptures of antiquity
and Italian art to develop a visual language
which could be deployed in historical
compositions of his own. Barry designed
a number of important history paintings
whilst in Italy including his great painting
of *The Education of Achilles* now in the Yale
Center for British Art. Whilst the painting,
which was exhibited at the Royal Academy
shortly after Barry's return to Britain in
1772, seems likely to have been painted in
London, the present important, previously
unpublished, preparatory drawing was
probably made in Italy. In its combination
of visual and literary sources, it represents
an extraordinary distillation of Barry's self-
conscious fashioning as a 'history painter'.[2]

The drawing is a fluid and confident
line study depicting his initial idea for the
Yale picture, which illustrates the story
of the young Achilles being instructed by
the centaur Chiron. Chiron was renowned
for his goodness and wisdom and was the
teacher of a number of celebrated heroes
in the classical world. Here he instructs the
youthful Achilles in the use of weapons,
in the arts, symbolized by the lyre, and
in mathematics, represented in the painting by a Eucledian diagram traced on the
ground at the end of Achilles' robe. As
William Pressly has pointed out, in spirit
Barry's picture is more closely attuned to
the tragic characterisation of the mature
Achilles found in Homer's *Iliad* rather than
to the less gloomy accounts of his early

education found in Pindar's *Third Nemean
Ode*, Statius' *Achilleid*, and Philostratus the
Elder's *Imagines*.[3] The present drawing offers
important evidence of Barry's initial idea
and significantly the sources of his inspiration for the composition.

Writing to Burke in April 1769 Barry
noted:

*The object of my studies is rather contracting
itself every day, and concentrating upon a few
principal things, compositions of one, or a few
figures, three or four at most, turning upon
some particular of beauty, distress, or some
other simple obvious thing, like what is to be
seen in the antique groups, or like what is told
of the Greek painters, which exactly corresponds
with what we find in the statues that remain
of them.*[4]

James Barry RA
*The Education of Achilles, c.*1772
Oil on canvas · 40½ × 50¾ inches · 1029 × 1289 mm
Yale Center for British Art, New Haven

J. Barry Invt.

Barry's contraction of ideas, his focus on 'compositions of one, or a few figures' and reliance on the works of 'Greek painters', perfectly describes his design for *The Education of Achilles*. Barry knew a celebrated ancient painting of the same subject-matter at Herculaneum, although he was actually critical of the fresco in a letter to Burke.[5] As William Pressly has pointed out Barry's immediate influence may have been a work by Pompeo Batoni although since this work was completed in the 1740s and housed in Lucca it seems more likely that Barry was looking at the works of a more conventionally celebrated master.[6] The figure of Achilles, seen almost in profile, is closely modeled on the figure of Apollo from the fresco of *Apollo and Marsyas* by Raphael painted on the ceiling of the Stanza della Segnatura. For Barry, Raphael was the ultimate model, and in the small panels on the ceiling of the Stanza della Segnatura he depicted: 'a few figures … turning upon some particular of beauty, distress or some

obvious thing.' For the figure of Chiron Barry turned to the two great sculptures in the Vatican collection: the *Laocoön* and *Belvedere Torso*, both believed in the eighteenth century to be the works of Greek sculptors.

Neither a prolific nor a particularly confident draughtsman, Barry made two preparatory studies for *The Education of Achilles*: the present sheet and a drawing now in the Ashmolean.[7] This underlines the importance of the composition to Barry's development as a 'history painter'. The present sheet is the most fully developed and ambitious of the two studies and is strikingly different from the finished painting, giving important insight into the gestation of the project. Barry has carefully delineated the musculature of Chiron's chest emphasizing its debt to the Belvedere Torso, whilst the figure of Achilles appears more mature and closer to Raphael's *Apollo* than the diminutive youth in the finished work. In the final painting Barry sets the figures in a landscape

diffusing the intensity and sculptural aspect of the group, perhaps suggesting a shift of emphasis that took place between Rome and London. Having two studies for the painting is rare and extremely revealing, underlining its importance to his future work.

Barry had heard news of the newly founded Royal Academy from amongst others its first President, Sir Joshua Reynolds, on his arrival in Rome. He must therefore have been alive to the importance of a new public forum for the exhibition of historical works in London and begun to prepare works specifically for this market and *The Education of Achilles* was amongst his earliest exhibits, being shown at the Academy in 1772. This sheet is therefore an important record of an early historical design by Barry made in preparation for perhaps the most significant painting of his early career.

NOTES

1   Edward Fryer, *The Works of James Barry*, London, 1809, I., pp.77–82 .

2   This sheet, despite being accessible in the collection of the academic Ralph Holland, was not included in any catalogue of Barry's drawings: Robert Wark, *James Barry*, unpublished PhD thesis, Harvard University, 1952; David Solkin, *The Drawings of James Barry*, unpublished MA thesis, Courtauld Institute of Art, University of London, 1974; *William* Pressly, *The Life and Art of James Barry*, New Haven and London, 1981.

3   William Pressly, *The Life and Art of James Barry*, New Haven and London, 1981, cat.no.,

4   Edward Fryer, *The Works of James Barry*, London, 1809, I., pp.158–64.

5   Edward Fryer, *The Works of James Barry*, London, 1809, I., pp.108–17.

6   William Pressly, *The Life and Art of James Barry*, New Haven and London, 1981, pp.35–6.

7   *William* Pressly, *The Life and Art of James Barry*, New Haven and London, 1981, cat.no.3, p.245.

James Barry RA
*Portraits of Barry and Burke in the characters of Ulysses and his companion fleeing from the cave of Polyphemus, c.*1776
Oil on canvas · 50 × 40⅛ inches · 1270 × 1020 mm
Crawford Art Gallery, Cork

Raphael
*Apollo and Marsyas, c.*1508–11
Fresco on the ceiling of the Stanza della Segnatura, Palace of the Vatican, Rome

LOUIS-GABRIEL BLANCHET 1705–1772

Portrait of a Gentleman

Oil on canvas
39 × 29 inches · 990 × 737 mm
Signed *L Blanchet*, upper left
Painted in the mid 1740s

EXHIBITED
London, Burlington Fine Arts Club,
*Exhibition of the French School of the 18th
Century*, 1913, no.63, as 'Cardinal York.'

During the eighteenth century portraiture in Rome developed a distinctive, cosmopolitan style as practitioners from outside the city dominated the field: the Frenchman Pierre Subleyras, the Lucchese Pompeo Batoni, the Bohemian Anton Raphael Mengs and Austrian Anton von Maron. One reason for this diversity was Rome's prominence as a place of artistic and educational pilgrimage for young artists and travellers from other European nations undertaking the 'Grand Tour'. The present exceptionally fine portrait is illustrative of the distinctive Roman style as well as the mode of 'Grand Tour' portraiture; made by the celebrated French portraitist Louis-Gabriel Blanchet, it probably depicts a foreign visitor to the city proudly holding a book, a prop suggestive of both learning and the implicit educational

function of travel in the mid-eighteenth century. Blanchet occupies an important – if now neglected – position in the development of portraiture in Rome during the first half of the eighteenth century and this portrait is a strikingly assured and finely executed example of his early work.[1]

Blanchet was born in Versailles in 1705, the son of a *valet de chambre* of Monsieur Blouin, himself the principal valet of Louis XIV.[2] In 1727 he won second place in the Prix de Rome competition, missing out on the first prize to his friend Pierre Subleyras. This success enabled him to move to Rome and study at the Académie de France à Rome, situated in Palazzo Mancini on the Corso, which was then under the direction of the painter Nicolas Vleughels. Blanchet's earliest dated portrait depicts Vleughels's brother-in-law, the Roman painter Giovanni Paolo Panini. The portrait of *Panini* which is dated 1736, demonstrates how Blanchet's earliest works were a careful combination of the rich palette of Italian Maratteschi painters, such as Marco Benefial and the grand visual language of Baroque French portraiture.

Blanchet soon established a thriving portrait practice and was encouraged by the patronage of the Duc de Saint-Aignan, the French ambassador, who had arrived in Rome in 1732.

Among the seven paintings acquired by the Duc de Saint-Aignan was the double portrait of *the Reverend Fathers François Jacquier and Thomas Leseur* of 1752 (Musée

Louis Gabriel Blanchet
Giovanni Paolo Panini, 1736
Private Collection
Courtesy of Colnaghi, London and Bernheimer, Munich

des Beaux Arts, Nantes), mathematicians who contributed to the scientific reputation of the Minim convent of S. Trinità, they are depicted amidst telescopes, an armillary sphere, and celestial globe. Blanchet's portraits of two rich Lyonese, the brothers *Claude Tolozan D'Amaranthe and Louis Tolozan de Montfort* of 1756 (Musée des Beaux-Arts, Lyon and The Walters Art Gallery, Baltimore), underline his elegant, luminous, and colourful style of painting.[3]

Blanchet is most famous for his portraits of members of the exiled Stuart Court. In 1736 he graduated from the Académie, but decided not to return to France, instead Blanchet remained in Rome; the annual census (Stati delle anime) reveal that he shared lodgings with Pierre Subleyras.[4] Following the death of the painter Antonio David in 1737, Blanchet was commissioned by King James III (the Old Pretender) to paint copies of portraits of his sons by Jean-Étienne Liotard.[5] This contact with the Stuart Court resulted in a number of commissions from other Jacobites resident in the city and probably brought Blanchet to the attention of other British Grand Tourists.[6]

Blanchet's portraits of the Stuart princes look similar to the work of his most celebrated contemporary, his friend and fellow Academician Pierre Subleyras. Subleyras arrived in Rome in 1728, having won first prize in the Prix de Rome in 1727, according to Vleughels's correspondence, he quickly distinguished himself as a portraitist also attracting the patronage of the Duc de Saint-Aignan.[7] A portrait he executed in

Pierre Subleyras
Horatio Walpole, 1st Earl of Orford, c.1746
Oil on canvas · 38 × 29 inches · 965 × 737 mm
© Leeds Museum and Art Galleries (Temple Newsam House) UK / The Bridgeman Art Library

Louis Gabriel Blanchet
Portrait of a gentleman, 1767
Oil on canvas
Musée des Beaux Art, Nîmes, France / Giraudon / The Bridgeman Art Library

1746–7 of the English Grand Tourist, *Horatio Walpole* (Temple Newsam House, Leeds) is particularly close in conception and handling to the present portrait. Walpole is shown seated at a table, his right hand resting on an open book and his left gesticulating out of the picture frame. Subleyras deploys the same stock devices of rich costume and, most tellingly, the ornate arm of a chair to frame the composition. The refined palette and exquisite handling are also similar in the two canvases, suggesting both a date range for the present picture and the visual context.

The present portrait – the sitter's identity, as with many of Blanchet's Roman works, is unknown – also shows strong similarities with Blanchet's earlier portrait of Panini, particularly in terms of the pose and handling. The sitter is shown seated facing to the right in a similar blue-coat with gold frogging, which contrasts to the voluminous russet cloak which suggests a classical Roman toga. As Bowron has noted writing about the portrait of Panini it is these elements which demonstrate: 'Blanchet's usual confident command of light, color and texture.'[8] This sitter's hand is shown resting on a book, but unlike in later portraits by Blanchet, the spine of the book is left blank and in contrast to his later works, the background is not ornamented with vegetation, antique sculpture or an interior view giving an unusual intensity to this work.[9]

Blanchet was in contact with a number of British painters and travellers outside the Jacobite court. In 1753 he painted a portrait of the architect *William Chambers*, shown in an oval with a number of architectural plans and books as well as a portrait of the Irish painter James Barry in 1766.[10] Blanchet

painted numerous English tourists, including a fine portrait of *Henry Willoughby, Lord Middleton* and *Henry, 8th Baron Arundell of Wardour*.[11] But Blanchet's greatest impact on British painters was through his innovative landscape drawing, he was one of a number of French painters living in Italy who pioneered the use of drawing plein air studies in black and white chalks on blue or grey paper, which had an enormous impact on artists such as Richard Wilson and his Danish follower Johan Mandelberg, whose portrait Blanchet painted (Royal Academy of Fine Arts, Copenhagen).

This accomplished portrait perfectly demonstrates the qualities which made the French painters trained in the 1720s the leading portraitists in Rome in the middle of the century. The masterful handling of costume demonstrates why the work of painters like Blanchet and Subleyras had such a great impact on their Italian contemporaries, particularly Pompeo Batoni. Although the sitter has not, so far, been identified, this painting is a highly stylish Grand Tour portrait and probably depicts a traveller in Rome.

NOTES

1 Blanchet has received only one dedicated scholarly article: Olivier Michel, 'Un pittore francese a Rome, Louis-Gabriel Blanchet', *Strenna dei romanisti*, 57, 1996, pp.467–86.

2 Ed. E P Bowron and J J Rishel, *Art in Rome in the Eighteenth Century*, exh.cat., Philadelphia (Philadelphia Museum of Art), 2000, pp.327–328.

3 Olivier Michel, 'Un pittore francese a Rome, Louis-Gabriel Blanchet', *Strenna dei romanisti*, 57, 1996, pp.470–472.

4 For Subleyras see: eds. Olivier Michel and Pierre Rosenberg, *Subleyras 1699–1749*, exh. cat. Paris (Louvre), 1987.

5 For Blanchet's work for the Stuarts see: Edward Corp, *The Stuarts in Italy; A Royal Court in Permanent Exile*, Cambridge, 2011, pp.285–303.

6 For the link between Stuart and British Grand Tour patronage see: Edward Corp, 'The Stuart Court and the Patronage of Portrait-Painters in Rome, 1717-57', in eds. David R. Marshall, Susan Russell and Karin Wolfe, *Roma Britannica: Art Patronage and Cultural Exchange in Eigtheenth-Century Rome*, London, 2011, p.46–47.

7 eds. Olivier Michel and Pierre Rosenberg, *Subleyras 1699–1749*, exh.cat. Paris (Louvre), 1987, pp.21–4.

8 Ed. E P Bowron and J J Rishel, *Art in Rome in the Eighteenth Century*, exh.cat., Philadelphia (Philadelphia Museum of Art), 2000, cat. no.182.

9 For example Blanchet's portrait of an unknown sitter in a private collection dated 1766 shows him holding a copy of the Dialogues of Phocion. See Francesco Petrucci, *Pittura di Ritratto a Roma: il '700*, Rome, 2010, II, p.437. Also the unknown portrait in a private collection, showing a sitter in a stone oval holding a copy of Bernard Forest de Bélidor's work on hydraulics. See Francesco Petrucci, *Pittura di Ritratto a Roma: il '700*, Rome, 2010, I, p.177.

10 See Francesco Petrucci, *Pittura di Ritratto a Roma: il '700*, Rome, 2010, I, p.176.

11 See *Pittura di Ritratto a Roma: il '700*, Rome, 2010, II, pp.438–439.

FRANCIS COTES RA 1726–1770

Mary Colebrooke, later Lady Aubrey (1750–1781)

Pastel
25½ × 29½ inches · 650 × 750 mm
Signed and dated *F Cotes pxt 1766*, lower left
In the original important English rococo frame.

COLLECTIONS
Probably Sir George Colebrooke, the sitter's uncle;
By descent, 2013.

LITERATURE
Neil Jeffares, *Dictionary of pastellists before 1800* (online edition).

John Finlayson, after Sir Joshua Reynolds
Miss Wynyard, 1771
Mezzotint · 19½ × 13⅝ inches · 498 × 348 mm
© The Trustees of the British Museum

With respect to Crayon Painting, *the present age has produced an uncommon instance of excellence in one of our own Countrymen. I mean the late Mr. Francis Cotes … it seems to be universally allowed by all good judges, that as a* Crayon Painter, *this celebrated Artist excelled most of his Contemporaries.*[1]

The spectacular, previously unpublished portrait of *Mary Colebrooke* is one of Francis Cotes's finest and most complex pastels, made at the height of his career. Signed and dated 1766 and housed in a magnificent English Rococo frame, the portrait remained unknown to scholars until 2013. Cotes, one of the most celebrated portraitists of the mid-century, a founder member of the Royal Academy and widely patronised by London society, was enjoying a reputation equal to that of Reynolds at the time of his premature death in 1770. As his pupil James Russell observed, it was 'universally allowed' that as a 'Crayon Painter', Cotes 'excelled most of his Contemporaries', who included Rosalba Carriera, Jean-Étienne Liotard and Jean Baptiste Perronneau. Although Russell's comments should be read as an assertion of Cotes's superiority over his British contemporaries, particularly Joshua Reynolds and Thomas Gainsborough something suggested by his magnificent portrait of *Mary Colebrooke*, in which Cotes proves that he was fully master of the 'Grand Manner' in pastel portraiture.

Born in London in 1726, Cotes was of Irish extraction (his father had been mayor of Galway in 1716). He spent his working life in Britain and was apprenticed to the successful portraitist and print-seller George Knapton in 1747. His earliest works appear similar in style and execution to those of

Knapton, and another of Knapton's pupils, Arthur Pond. By 1763 Cotes's had established a successful portrait practice, enabling him to take a lease on a house at 32 Cavendish Square. Situated on the south side of the square, it was described in the sale catalogue after his death as a 'Large and commodious House, with an elegant Suite of Five Rooms on the First Floor, and Coach Houses and Stabling.'[2] The house, located in a fashionable part of London, was remodelled by Cotes to include, in addition to his own studio, a room for pupils to paint in, and a gallery or 'Shew Room'. It was from this address that Cotes is listed exhibiting at the Society of Artists throughout the 1760s and the present picture may well be identifiable as the 'portrait of a lady; in crayons' he exhibited in 1766.[3]

An unusually large and ambitious pastel, it shows the sitter, Mary Colebrooke, eldest daughter of Sir James Colebrooke, aged 16 in a landscape leaning against a herm of Flora. Cotes has dressed *Mary Colebrooke* in loose, classicising costume: a pink shift, tied with a blue and yellow sash and adorned at the sleeves with elaborate jewels. Cotes used the same costume for his portrait of *Mrs Child* exhibited at the Society of Artists the same year and now in the collection of the Earl of Jersey.[4] The modish pose, setting and costume were staples of fashionable portraiture in the mid-1760s. The idea of posing a beautiful young sitter in a sylvan landscape, with the suggestion of a classical setting – in the form of the sculpted herm – was one that had been made fashionable by Joshua Reynolds. In the same year Reynolds produced a portrait of *Emily Wynyard* which is strikingly similar to Cotes's portrait. Around 1766 Cotes produced some of

his most spectacular works in pastel. The present highly sophisticated composition can be compared with the portrait of *Frances Ann Hoare* at Stourhead, Wiltshire. The composition, scale and approach all suggest that the present work should be viewed as one of Cotes's most accomplished and successful pastel portraits.

In his *Elements of Painting with Crayons*, published in 1777, John Russell outlined the method of executing pastel portraits he learnt from Cotes. We therefore have a remarkable explication of Cotes's working practice. In line with contemporary painting, the 'attitude' of the sitter was essential, 'if a young Lady, express more vivacity than in the majestic beauty of a middle-aged Woman.'[5] Cotes has accordingly portrayed *Mary Colebrooke* outside, her hand casually holding a flower and resting on the herm of Flora.

After explaining the rudiments of preparing the paper, which was generally blue in colour and supported on canvas, Russell discusses the method of taking the likeness: beginning with a sketch, before laying in the features. This having been completed, the painter uses a: '*Crayon* of pure Carmine' to 'carefully draw the Nostril and Edge of the Nose, next the shadow, then, with the faintest Carmine Teint, lay in the highest light upon the Nose and Forehead, which must be executed broad.' Once this 'dead-colouring' was finished, the painter was instructed to 'sweeten the whole together, by rubbing it over with his finger.' Then the background was added, applied only very thinly closest to the head, to aid the illusion of volume, and finally the finishing 'teints': 'vermillion' on the forehead; the cheeks 'a few touches of the orange-coloured *Crayon*' and for the

Francis Cotes
Frances Ann Acland, Lady Hoare, 1735–6
Pastel
29½ × 25½ inches · 750 × 647 mm
Stourhead House, Wiltshire
© National Trust / David Cousins

Francis Cotes
Joseph Gulston and his brother John Gulston, 1754
Pastel
26½ × 32½ inches · 674 × 825 mm
The J. Paul Getty Museum, Los Angeles

eyes 'the most difficult feature to execute', he advised using a sharpened pastel and the 'finger as little as possible'. All these characteristic elements can be seen masterfully deployed by Cotes in his portrait of *Mary Colebrooke*.

Edward Edwards recorded that Cotes charged 'twenty guineas for a three-quarter, forty for a half-length, and eighty for a whole length'; as Edward Johnson has pointed out 'three-quarter length' refers to pictures 30 × 25in.[6] According to Edwards the present portrait would therefore have cost 20 guineas, although the archival evidence of other portraits of the same date suggest it would have been slightly more. In line with other pastellists of the period, Cotes would have offered frames and glasses at an additional cost. The evidence suggests that Cotes generally supplied three types of frame: a standard Carlo Maratta pattern; an English Palladian frame and a French-inspired rococo frame, which as Jacob Simon has pointed out, was an anglicised version of the type favoured by Jean-Étienne Liotard.[7] This last type – which Cotes used for his portrait of *Frances Hoare* – was notably less decorated than the frame Cotes used for the portrait of *Mary Colebrooke*. Whilst the general pattern is the same, it has been embellished with carved floral swags of outstanding quality and the punched profile is sculpted to a far higher standard suggesting the frame-maker was instructed directly by the patron rather than Cotes. In this case, this is likely to have been the sitter's uncle, Sir George Colebrook of Gatton Park in Surrey.

Francis Cotes
Lieut-Col the Hon Edmund Cragg Nugent, 1748
Pastel · 23¼ × 17¼ inches · 590 × 437 mm
Morgan Library & Museum, New York,
formerly with Lowell Libson Ltd

This newly discovered portrait of *Mary Colebrook* is a magnificent essay in Cotes's ability as a pastellist executed when he was at the height of his powers. The virtuosic range of his technique and sophistication of his approach – deploying the fashionable language of 'Grand Manner' portraiture – makes it one of Cotes's finest works. Housed in a frame of the highest quality, the portrait exemplifies Cotes's own observation that: 'Crayon pictures, when finely painted, are superlatively beautiful, and decorative in a very high degree.'[8]

We are grateful to Jacob Simon and Neil Jeffares for their help in cataloguing this portrait.

NOTES

1   J. Russell, *Elements of Painting with Crayons*, London, 1777, p.ii.
2   Edward Mead Johnson, *Francis Cotes: Complete Edition with a Critical Essay and a Catalogue*, Oxford, 1976, p.156.
3   Algernon Graves, *The Society of Great Britain 1760–1791; The Free Society of Artists 1761–1783, A Complete Dictionary of Contributors and their work from the Foundation of the Societies to 1791*, Bath, 1907, no.30, p.65.
4   Edward Mead Johnson, *Francis Cotes: Complete Edition with a Critical Essay and a Catalogue*, Oxford, 1976, No.190.
5   John Russell, *Elements of Painting with Crayons*, London, 1772, p.22.
6   Edward Mead Johnson, *Francis Cotes: Complete Edition with a Critical Essay and a Catalogue*, Oxford, 1976, p.17.
7   Jacob Simon, *The Art of the Picture Frame: Artist's, Patrons and the Framing of Portraits in Britain*, London, 1996, p.94.
8   Francis Cotes, 'Crayon Painting', *The European Magazine*, February 1797, p.84.

ALEXANDER COZENS 1717–1786

A small pool with willow trees

Brown washes on laid paper
8 × 11½ inches · 208 × 291 mm
Signed on original mount lower left:
Alex.r Cozens
Drawn *circa* 1770.

COLLECTIONS
Miss Aynscombe, niece of George
Challoner;
Katherine Townshend, her cousin, who
married the Rev. Thomas Bisse;
Col. T.-C. Bisse Challoner (1789–1872), son of
the above, who married Henrietta de Salis;
The Rev. H. J. de Salis (1828–1915), brother-in-
law of the above;
Major O. J. de Salis, great grandson of the
above, 1982;
Leger Galleries, London, 1982;
H. L. Dannhauser, to 2013.

EXHIBITED
London, Leger Galleries, *English
Watercolours*, December 1982, no.1, repr.

In an age addicted to the systematisation
of the natural sciences Alexander Cozens's
preoccupation was paradoxically seen as
both unexceptional and obsessional as his
friend, patron and pupil William Beckford

when speaking of Cozens noted that he was
'Almost as full of Systems as the Universe'.
The complicating factor was the number
of variables which he developed during
a long career which saw the publication
of only a few elements of his philosophy
regarding the aesthetics of nature and its
depiction. Indeed, one subscriber to his 1778
'Principles of Beauty', was to write hoping
that "it has spoke more intelligibly to you
than it seems to do to most people".[1] In the
headings that Cozens was to produce for his
1759 'The Various Species of Composition
of Landscape' he was to list no.12 as *A
lake, or a piece of water*. This was further
elucidated by the Rev Charles Davy in his
digest of Cozens's system made for Sir
George Beaumont as a 'flat ground or water
surrounded in Taste'.

In spite of the apparent complexity of
his theories Cozens enjoyed his activities
as a drawing master and had a large and
loyal roster of clients throughout his career.
Cozens's ultimate importance, for he
inspired no 'school' of professional follow-
ers other than his son, was his influence
on more than a generation of collectors

and arbiters of taste through his teaching
activities. In 1757 Edmund Burke published
what was perhaps the most important work
of the period on aesthetics, his 'Philosophical
Enquiry into the Origins of our Ideas of the
Sublime and Beautiful' and it was this work
that helped Alexander and subsequently his
son, John Robert, to develop a visual language
to convey the emotional responses that Burke
discoursed on.

The present drawing executed, entirely
with the brush in brown ink, is typical of
the 'beautiful' effects that Cozens strove to
achieve through the dynamics of a balanced
composition. John Robert Cozens was to
develop his father's aesthetics specifically in
the treatment of trees within the landscape
in the soft-ground etchings of 1789 published
as *Delineations of the General Character
Ramifications and Foliage of Forest Trees*.
Cozens's influence can especially be seen
in the work of Gainsborough who would
undoubtedly have had access to Alexander
Cozens's work.

1   Harriet Lister to John Grimston, Grimston
papers, Humberside County Record Office,
42/28.

John Robert Cozens, *Castel Gandolfo, c.*1780
Pencil · 5⅛ × 7⅜ inches · 130 × 187 mm
Yale Center for British Art, Paul Mellon Collection,
New Haven

Alexander Cozens, *Study of two willows, c.*1760
Black and brown inks, varnished
4 × 6⅜ inches · 102 × 162 mm
Yale Center for British Art, Paul Mellon Collection, New Haven

Thomas Gainsborough, *Landscape with three
cows in centre, amongst trees,* mid to late 1780s
Sugar-lift aquatint, printed in grey ink
© The Trustees of the British Museum

Alex.ʳ Cozens.

JOHN ROBERT COZENS 1752–1797

On the Arve in Savoy

Watercolour over pencil
9¼ × 14¼ inches · 238 × 363 mm
Signed lower left: *J. Cozens*
Inscribed on the original mount:
On the Arve in Savoy
Painted *circa* 1776

COLLECTIONS
Professor J. H. Abram
Norman D. Newall;
and by descent, 1979;
Private collection, 2013.

LITERATURE
C. F. Bell and T. Girtin, 'The Drawings
and Sketches of John Robert Cozens',
Walpole Society, Vol. XXIII, 1935, no.4ii.

EXHIBITED
Manchester, Whitworth Art Gallery,
*Watercolour Drawings by J. R. Cozens and
J. S. Cotman*, 1937, no.47.

This atmospheric Alpine view was painted during John Robert Cozens's first, hugely influential Continental trip. Travelling in the company of the great collector and connoisseur Richard Payne Knight, Cozens set out for Italy in August 1776, first undertaking a short Alpine tour. It was in the monumental landscape of the Alps, that Cozens saw at first hand the ideas of the sublime in nature which he had learnt from his artist father, Alexander Cozens and other theorists, such as Edmund Burke. The watercolours Cozens produced over his two months in France and Switzerland are regarded as some of the most compelling of the eighteenth century and as Kim Sloan has noted, in them:
Cozens had finally lifted watercolour painting out of the topographical recording of nature, to a new level where it was capable of fulfilling the serious intentions of art as oil painting.[1]

Cozens and Payne Knight followed a typical round trip from Geneva which included visiting Bonneville, Cluse, Sallanches, Mont Blanc, Chamonix and Martigny. In a contemporary guidebook, the area was described in the following terms:
The overhanging rocks of a prodigious height, and torrents pouring down in sheets from their very summits, are such wonders of Nature, as it is impossible to look upon without a mixture of astonishment and awe.[2]

This combination of 'astonishment and awe' were precisely the feelings Cozens captured in the views he made for Payne Knight. The present sheet shows a view on the river Arve in Savoy close to the town of Sallanches. It is based on one of the watercolours Cozens made for Payne Knight which later passed to the British Museum. The British Museum drawing is inscribed on the back: 'Banks of the Arve near Salinche

in Savoy/August 26 – 1776', making it one of Cozens's earliest Alpine views.[3] As Kim Sloan has noted: 'upon entering the Arve valley lined with mountains … Cozens immediately seems to have found the landscape which evoked a strong personal response.'[4] Cozens has taken evident delight in the towering rock formations on the right of the composition, placing the escarpment almost at the top of the composition, encroaching far into the space generally reserved for the sky. The view shows a debt to Alexander Cozens's theory of composition which demanded that masses should alternate on either side, thus the peaks on the left are shown as lower and less densely vegetated.[5] The economic, almost monochrome palette adds to the drama of the scene, giving the masses of the mountains an almost menacing quality.

The present drawing is probably a slightly later version made by Cozens either *en route* to Italy or once he was installed in Rome. Recent work has shown that very few watercolours were made 'on the spot' by British artists travelling on the Continent and from the visual evidence it seems likely that Cozens's alpine watercolours were based on a series of drawings which no longer survive.[6] But rather than detracting from the atmosphere or verisimilitude of the sheets, this detachment serves to amplify the initial response to the landscape. Cozens was deeply affected by the sublime nature of the Alpine scenery, but he mediated his response through the compositional theories of his father and contemporary literary and poetic associations. Thus the finished watercolours, produced in his studio in Rome, become a more concentrated expression of his

On the Arve in Savoy.

memories on seeing the original scenery and a clearer record of the emotions he felt. In the present watercolour – and the surviving Payne Knight sheet to which it is related – Cozens has heightened the escarpment on the right to add to the sense of 'astonishment and awe'.

Preserved in its original wash-lined mount, the present drawing is an important and beautiful example from Cozens's first great series of landscape watercolours. A visual essay on responses to the sublime in nature, Cozens's *View on the Arve* and other sheets from this Alpine trip, had an enormous impact upon the next generation of landscape artists in Britain, including J.M.W. Turner and Thomas Girtin.

John Robert Cozens
Banks of the Arve near Sallanches in Savoy, 1776
Watercolour · 9 × 13⅝ inches · 229 × 347 mm
Inscribed and dated verso
© The Trustees of the British Museum

NOTES

1 Kim Sloan, *Alexander and John Robert Cozens: The Poetry of* Landscape, New Haven and London, 1986, p.125.

2 M. Bourrit, trans. C. Davy, *A Relation of a Journey to the Glaciers in the Dutchy of Savoy*, Norwich, 1776, p.2.

3 In their chronological catalogue of Cozens's drawings, C.F. Bell and Thomas Girtin list it as number four. See C. F. Bell and T. Girtin, 'The Drawings and Sketches of John Robert Cozens', *Walpole Society*, Vol. XXIII, 1935, no.4i.

4 Kim Sloan, *Alexander and John Robert Cozens: The Poetry of* Landscape, New Haven and London, 1986, p.118.

5 Kim Sloan, *Alexander and John Robert Cozens: The Poetry of* Landscape, New Haven and London, 1986, pp.36–62.

6 For a discussion of the Alpine material see: Kim Sloan, *Alexander and John Robert Cozens: The Poetry of Landscape*, New Haven and London, 1986, p.115–116.

John Robert Cozens
Between Sallanches and Servoz, Mont Blanc in the distance, 1776
Watercolour · 9⅛ × 13⅞ inches · 232 × 352 mm
Dated and numbered verso
© The Trustees of the British Museum

JOHN ROBERT COZENS 1752–1797

The approach to Martigny, Rhone valley, Valais

Watercolour over pencil
19⅜ × 26¾ inches · 493 × 680 mm
Signed on the remains of the original
mount: *Jn Cozens*
Painted *circa* 1790

COLLECTIONS
Sir Frederick Eden;
By descent to Mrs Deverell;
Sir William Eden;
Norman D. Newall, 1979;
Private collection, 1985;
Miss D. Scharf.

LITERATURE
C. F. Bell and T. Girtin, 'The Drawings and
Sketches of John Robert Cozens', *Walpole
Society*, Vol. XXIII, 1935, no.12ii;
C. F. Bell, 'Additions and corrections to the
catalogue of sketches and drawings', *Walpole
Society*, 1947, p.5;
A. Wilton, *The Art of Alexander and John
Robert Cozens*, exh.cat. New Haven, 1980,
(Yale Center for British Art), p.50.

EXHIBITED
Manchester, Whitworth Art Gallery,
*Watercolour Drawings by J. R. Cozens and
J. S. Cotman*, 1937, no.86;
Newcastle-upon-Tyne, Laing Art Gallery,
Coronation Exhibition, 1953, no.28.

Most British travellers to Italy during the eighteenth century went overland, crossing the Alps at Mont Cenis, rather than risking the journey by sea. The landscape of Switzerland therefore formed an essential component of the Grand Tour. It is not surprising therefore to find that from the mid-century the spectacular scenery began to receive attention from travelling English writers, philosophers and, most impressively, painters. In 1770 William Pars produced a series of watercolours of a Swiss tour he undertook with his patron Henry Temple, 2nd Viscount Palmerston, and in 1776 John Robert Cozens set out for Italy with the connoisseur Richard Payne Knight. Whilst Pars's somewhat pedantic views betray their purpose as scientific observations, Cozens's alpine views, made in the company of Payne Knight fully embody in their breadth, drama and atmosphere the proto-Romantic fascination with the sublime.[1]

The present monumental sheet is a version of Cozens's most successful and enduring Alpine view. Depicting the Rhone Valley in the canton of Valais, near Geneva, this watercolour perfectly embodies the emotional response to landscape articulated by the Irish politician and philosopher Edmund Burke. In his 1757 treatise, *A Philosophical Enquiry into the Origin of Our Ideas of the Sublime and Beautiful*, Burke noted in a section on 'vastness':
I am apt to imagine likewise, that height is less grand than depth; and that we are more struck at looking down from a precipice, than looking up at an object of equal height.[2]

This idea of an instinctive response to landscape that was not classically 'picturesque' but nevertheless inspired great feeling formed the bedrock of Cozens's response

to Continental scenery. In the binary established by Burke, Cozens's views nearly always address the sublime rather than the beautiful.[3] Here the small Swiss dwellings and tiny group of mounted figures in the foreground are dwarfed by the monumental landscape, the towering escarpment to the right and the expanse of the Rhone Valley dissolving towards the distant mountains.

Whilst Burke's influence may account for the intellectual context for Cozens's view, compositionally it owes a great deal to the work of his father, Alexander Cozens. Alexander Cozens had made his own pioneering Grand Tour in 1746 and articulated his own approach to the art of composition in his *Various Species of Landscape* of 1760. Cozens senior attempted to reduce all nature to a series of general landscape types, or 'species' for the use of the artist.[4] In the present work, John Robert Cozens has used his father's general compositional plans, neatly framing the view of the Rhone Valley with the massed hills to the right and the clump of trees to the left and deliberately emphasising the meander of the river below to suggest distance. But unlike his father, who was not interested in topography, John Robert Cozens remained highly attuned to the realities of the landscape he portrayed. Indeed his genius lay in his ability to transmute topographical studies into highly evocative and poetic essays on the sublime.

The present watercolour is based on a large squared pencil study, dated August 30th 1776, which formed part of a volume entitled *28 sketches by J. Cozens of Views in Italy* now in the Sir John Soane's Museum, London. The Soane Museum study is inscribed '*Approach to Martinach Pais de Vallais*' and was made on the spot, whilst he was travelling to Italy

in the company of Richard Payne Knight.
A smaller wash drawing derived from this
in the Leeds City Art Gallery bears the
inscription: '*Pais de Vallais / near the Lake
Geneva*'. This information suggests that
the scene depicts a southward view of the
valley between the east end of the lake and
Martigny, where the travellers are likely to
have turned up the valley towards the north-
east, in the direction of Sion, capital of the
canton. An old label formerly attached to the
mount read: *The Valley of Sion, Switzerland*,
but this is likely to be a misconception as
two of Cozens's other versions of the view
show the sun centrally placed, high in the
sky, consistent with the southerly direction.

Made at the beginning of their tour
together, Cozens must have be conscious
of the marketability of his Italian views
carefully preparing the squared drawing for
use in making a finished watercolour, either
once settled in Rome or back in Britain.
On the back of the Soane drawing Cozens
made a list of the eight names of patrons
who commissioned finished watercolours of
this subject along with the price, 18 guineas
each.[5] Bell and Girtin suggest the list was
compiled over a period of time. The patrons
listed are: Sir R. Hoare, Mr Windham,
Mr Wigstead, Mr Sunderland, Mr Chalie,
Dr Chelsum, Mr Walwin and Sir Frederick
Eden.[6]

With the exception of the watercolour
presented here, and the one commissioned
by Sir Richard Colt Hoare, none of the
others can be traced back to the collectors
in Cozens's list. The present work is the
largest, and only signed example of the
seven variants of this composition. A label
previously attached to the reverse of this
watercolour read *Cozens or Payne/Belonged to*

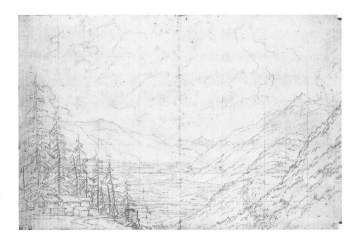

John Robert Cozens
*Approach to Martinach Pais
de Vallais*
Pencil, squared up for copying
9 × 14¼ inches · 229 × 362 mm
Dated August 30, 1776
By courtesy of the Trustees
of Sir John Soane's Museum,
London

John Robert Cozens
Pays de Valais
Pen and ink, blue and grey
wash over pencil
13 × 20½ inches · 332 × 522 mm
© Fitzwilliam Museum,
Cambridge

John Robert Cozens
The Pays de Valais
Watercolour, pencil and red-
brown gouache
14¼ × 20½ inches · 362 × 521 mm
Yale Center for British Art, Paul
Mellon Collection, New Haven

my Father / Given me by Mrs Deverell. Another Cozens watercolour also formerly in the collection of N. D. Newall was also inscribed on a label in the same hand as belonging to Mrs Deverell and signed by William Eden. It was acquired by Newall at the same time and from the same source as the present watercolour. It seems likely, therefore, that the William Eden was Sir William Eden, 4th Bt the second son of Sir Frederick Morton Eden, 2nd Bt. Sir Frederick Morton Eden made a journey to Italy in 1790 and, very likely ordered this view from Cozens on his return, the artist adding his name to those who had already acquired versions.[7]

In spite of his short career, John Robert Cozens developed the theoretical exercises of his father into what John Constable, when speaking of his work, characterized as 'poetry'.[8] A poetic conception of landscape which had a transformative impact upon the work of the next generation of British watercolourists, particularly J.M.W. Turner and Thomas Girtin who both copied Cozens's work under the supervision of Dr Thomas Munro. This monumental work, preserved in its original mount which is inscribed on the bottom left 'Jn Cozens', was made when he was at the height of his powers. It perfectly captures the poetic appeal which fired the imagination of the later generation of British landscape artists, whilst also remaining one of the quintessential images of the Grand Tour.

BELL & GIRTIN CATALOGUE NO.12

i.   Monochrome ink and wash drawing,
     7⅜ × 10⅝ inches,
     Collection: Leeds City Art Gallery
     (Lupton Bequest)

ii. 19⅜ × 26½ inches,
     Collection: formerly Norman D. Newall;
     The present work.

iii. 17¾ × 25 inches,
     Collection: Sir Richard Colt Hoare; by descent,
     Stourhead, Wiltshire.

iv. 16¼ × 25 inches,
     Collection: City of Birmingham Art Gallery.

v.   15¼ × 20¾ inches,
     Collection: Fitzwilliam Museum, Cambridge.

vi. 16¾ × 24½ inches,
     Collection: formerly, Victor Rienaecker.

vii. Squared-up pencil study.
     Inscribed: *Approach to Martinach Pais de Vallais*,
     Dated: August 30, 1776,
     Collection: Sir John Soane's Museum, London.

Another large version (14⅛ × 20½ inches) not listed in Bell and Girtin, was owned by the Littlewood family and subsequently purchased by Paul Mellon, (Yale Center for British Art, New Haven, Paul Mellon collection).

NOTES

1 For Pars see Andrew Wilton, *Journey through the Alps*, 1979.
2 Edmund Burke, *A Philosophical Inquiry into the Sublime and Beautiful*, Abingdon, 2008, p.72.
3 Kim Sloan, *Alexander and John Robert Cozens: the Poetry of Landscape*, New Haven and London, 1986, pp.107–108.
4 Kim Sloan, *Alexander and John Robert Cozens: the Poetry of Landscape*, New Haven and London, 1986, pp.36–61.
5 Paul Oppé, *Alexander and John Robert Cozens*, London, 1952, p.132.
6 C.F. Bell and T. Girtin, 'The Drawings and Sketches of John Robert Cozens', *The Walpole Society*, 23, p.29.
7 Andrew Wilton, *The Art of Alexander and John Robert Cozens*, exh.cat. New Haven (Yale Center for British Art), p.50.
8 Charles Leslie, *Memoirs of John Constable*, London, 1845, p.89.

ARTHUR DEVIS 1712–1787

A Roman Capriccio

Oil on canvas
24⅜ × 29 inches · 620 × 737 mm
Signed and dated *ADevis 1736*, lower centre

COLLECTIONS
Probably Anthony Devis, half-brother of
Arthur Devis;
Ellin Devis, Arthur Devis's daughter, a gift
from the above;
Ellin Devis Marris, adopted daughter of the
above, by bequest in 1820;
Arthur Tooth & Sons Ltd (as by Panini);
Private collection, UK, 1987;
The Leger Galleries, 1987;
The Hon. Simon Sainsbury, acquired from
the above in 1987;
Sainsbury sale, Christie's, 18th June 2008,
lot 205 [the literature cited incorrectly in
Christie's catalogue entry applies to the
painting listed by D'Oench (1979) as no.272];
Private collection, 2013

LITERATURE
Ellen Gates D'Oench, *Arthur Devis (1712–1787)*;
Master of the Georgian Conversation Piece,
A Dissertation Presented to the Faculty of
the Graduate School of Yale University in
Candidacy for the Degree of Doctor of
Philosophy, 1979, cat.no.272.

Arthur Devis is best known as a master of
conversation pieces and full-length portraits
in small scale, described by Sacheverell
Sitwell as 'the perfect small master of the
school.'[1] His work as a painter of landscapes and architectural capriccios is less
well known. This previously unpublished
ruinscape, made in the manner of Giovanni
Paolo Panini, sheds important light on
his early career and crucially, his working
methods. Signed and dated 1736, Devis
evidently retained an affection for the painting, incorporating it into at least two of his
interior conversation pieces. This catalogue
entry contains important new information
on Devis's early career and art training in the
north-west of Britain in the 1730s, as well as
reproducing extracts from the unpublished
will of Devis's daughter.

Born in Preston, Lancashire, in 1712
Devis's early training took place in the
north-west where he worked with the
Flemish painter Peter Tillemans. Tillemans
seems to have spent time at Knowsley
Hall in Lancashire in 1728–9, completing a
number of spectacular landscapes depicting
the house, park and James Stanley, 10th Earl
of Derby's racecourse.[2] It is clear from the

Hamlet Winstanley,
Capriccio with Castel Sant'Angelo
Pen and ink on paper, *c.*1725
Warrington Museum and Art Gallery, Warrington

surviving correspondence of the 10th Earl
that Knowsley, with its substantial collection of old master paintings, became an
important base for artists in the region.[3]
We know at least one other of Tillemans's
pupils, Edward Coppock, stayed at Knowsley
learning to draw, and in 1736 George Stubbs
arrived to copy paintings supervised by his
master, Hamlet Winstanley. According to
Stubbs's earliest biographer, Ozias Humphry,
the first picture he attempted to copy at
Knowsley was a ruinscape by Giovanni
Paolo Panini.[4]

It is highly suggestive that at the same
date Devis was also completing a work
strongly influenced by the Italian painter
Panini. Further investigation reveals that
the present painting, which is not a copy of
any existing Panini design, but is in fact a
composition directly derived from a drawing
by Hamlet Winstanley that is contained in a
sketchbook now in the Warrington Museum
and Art Gallery. Winstanley had visited
Italy in 1723–1725 and filled a sketchbook
with topographical landscape drawings
and subsequently produced a number of
capriccio studies derived from these accurate
drawings. One such sheet depicts the Castel
Sant'Angelo behind a classical church and
campanile identical to the buildings on the
right hand side of Devis's painting. Devis's
use of such an idiosyncratic set of structures seems certain to have derived from
Winstanley's drawing adding further to the
supposition that Devis trained at Knowsley
and continued to have contact there
throughout his early years in nearby Preston.

Turning to the painting itself, it appears
to be a conventional digest of classic Roman
monuments, arranged to form a fanciful
ruinscape. On the far left of the composition

are the three columns of the Temple of
Castor and Pollux from the Forum in Rome;
in the left foreground is the remains of a
torso of Venus; prominently in the background is Trajan's Column and behind it the
dome of Santa Maria di Loreto; to the right
a profile of the Capitoline and on the far
right the group of buildings borrowed from
Winstanley's drawing. Standing amongst
the ruins are a group of figures, in vaguely
classical costume, in discussion. The works
of Giovanni Paolo Panini were extremely
fashionable amongst British collectors from
the mid-1730s onwards, Devis's painting and
more importantly his conduit, in the form
of Winstanley's Italian drawings, represent a
very early instance of British artists imitat-
ing this format. In the following generation
countless British painters would replicate
Panini's designs as decorative additions to
interiors as new Palladian designs demanded
painted overmantels and overdoors, but
Devis's signed and dated composition was
absolutely at the forefront of this fashion.

Given the squareish format of the present
painting it seems likely that it was designed
as an overdoor. This is confirmed by Devis's
inclusion of elements from the present
composition in at least two of his earliest
conversation pieces. The profile of the three
columns from the Temple of Castor and
Pollux, Venus's torso and standing figures
are visible in a painting placed above a
door on the right-hand side of Devis's early
masterpiece the *Crewe Conversation Piece*.
Painted in about 1742, it is widely regarded
as Devis's most important early work.[5]
The present painting is also visible hanging over the mantelpiece in his painting of
William Atherton and his Wife Lucy (Walker
Art Gallery, Liverpool). D'Oench raised the
possibility that this view may relate to a
work by Devis, but did not explicitly link it
with the present painting despite the picture
hanging in the *Atherton Conversation Piece*
precisely replicating the right-hand side of
the present composition.[6] The existence of
another ruinscape by Devis in the manner of

Arthur Devis
*The Crewe conversation piece, c.*1742,
and detail (right)
Oil on canvas · 32⅜ × 40 inches · 823 × 1017 mm
Private collection

Arthur Devis
Classical ruins with figures
Oil on canvas · 21 × 28½ inches · 532 × 724 mm
Signed and dated 1736
Whereabouts unknown (London art market, 1939)

Arthur Devis
William Atherton and his wife Lucy, c.1743
Oil on canvas · 36¼ × 50 inches · 920 × 1270 mm
Courtesy National Museums Liverpool

Panini of a similar size, also signed and dated 1736 (last recorded on the London market in 1939),[7] makes it highly likely that the present picture is the one of the pair mentioned in the will of Devis's daughter, Ellin Devis:
2 Ruins of Rome after Panini painted in the [first] part of my d^r ffathers life and given to me by my uncle Anth^y.[8]

Anthony Devis was Arthur Devis's younger half-brother; he practiced as a landscape painter in Preston and later London and may have retained the two *capricci* paintings when Arthur moved to London in 1742. Other than nine landscape works in watercolour by Devis included in Tillemans's sale in 1733 – which included copies after van Bloemen, Panini and Ricci and all remain untraced – no other imitations or copies by Devis are known strengthening the identification of our picture as one of those mentioned in Ellin Devis's will.[9]

Exceptionally finely executed, this painting is important for our understanding of Devis's early career. It raises the possibility of his contact with Hamlet Winstanley in about 1736 – and therefore with George Stubbs – giving a context for his early work at Knowsley and is a crucial clue in understanding his work as a painter of decorative overdoors. Its presence in Ellin Devis's will and appearance in a number of his most significant early composition also underscores the importance of the work to Devis himself. For an ambitious and highly talented artist competing for patronage in London in the 1740s without having travelled to Italy it would have served as a powerful testament of his Continental sophistication and abilities to master fashionable Italianate models.

NOTES

1 Sacheverell Sitwell, *Conversation Pieces: A Survey of English Domestic Portraits and their Painters*, London, 1969, p.54.
2 Ellen D'Oench, *Arthur Devis (1712–1787); Master of the Georgian Conversation Piece*, A Dissertation Presented to the Faculty of the Graduate School of Yale University in Candidacy for the Degree of Doctor of Philosophy, 1979, p.25.
3 Francis Russell, 'The Derby Collection (1721–1735)', *The Walpole Society*, vol. 53, 1987, p.143–180.
4 Judy Egerton, *George Stubbs, Painter*, New Haven and London, 2007, p.13.
5 Ellen D'Oench, *The Conversation Piece: Arthur Devis & His Contemporaries*, exh.cat. New Haven (Yale Center for British Art), 1980, p.21.
6 Ellen D'Oench, *The Conversation Piece: Arthur Devis & His Contemporaries*, exh.cat. New Haven (Yale Center for British Art), 1980, cat.no.11, p.48. This idea is repeated, although not elaborated on, in: Alex Kidson, *Earlier British Paintings in the Walker Art Gallery and Sudley House*, Liverpool, 2013, p.34.
7 Current whereabouts unknown, formerly with Christie's, 12 May 1939, lot 107.
8 Kew, Public Record Office, Prob 11/1626.
9 Mr Cock's, April 19–20, 1733, lots 262–60. See: R.Raines, 'Peter Tillemans Life and Work', *The Walpole Society*, 1978, 47, pp.34–38.

JOHN FLAXMAN RA 1755–1826

The Adoration of the Magi

Marble
9 × 17 inches · 228 × 430 mm
Executed *circa* 1792–94

COLLECTIONS
Private collection, since 2003

EXHIBITED
Oxford, Ashmolean Museum, 2006 – 2008,
on loan;
London, Tate Britain, *Return of the Gods*,
2008, no.9;
Berlin, Skulpturensammlung und Museum
für Byzantaninische Kunst Staatliche
Museen, *John Flaxman und die Renaissance;
Ein Meister des Klassizismus im Dialog Masaccio
und Donatello*, 2009, no.8.

LITERATURE
David Bindman, 'John Flaxman's Adoration
of the Magi Rediscovered', *Apollo*, 162,
no.526, 2005, pp.40–45.;
Marjorie Trusted, *The Return of the Gods,
Neoclassical Sculpture in Britain*, exhibition
catalogue, London, 2008, p.25;
Sylvie Tritz and Hans-Ulrich Kessler, *John
Flaxman und die Renaissance; Ein Meister des
Klassizismus im Dialog Masaccio und Donatello*,
exhibition catalogue, Berlin, 2009, pp.64–75.

This remarkable relief sculpture looks, at first sight, as though it was made in the twentieth century: the purity and economy of line produces an abstraction of form wholly without precedent in relief sculpture of the eighteenth century. Carved by John Flaxman in Rome sometime between 1792 and his departure in 1794, it represents a startling distillation of his fascination with both Greek art – particularly vase painting – and the sculpture and painting of the Italian *quattrocento*. Scholars have long discerned these influences in Flaxman's pioneering illustrations to Homer and Dante, the publication of which represented a watershed in the development of European Neo-Classicism, but it is only with the recent rediscovery of the present relief that their full realisation in his sculpture can be appreciated. As such, this highly personal and intimate piece deserves not only a place as one of Flaxman's most important works in marble, but as one of the most sophisticated and extraordinary sculptures made in late eighteenth-century Europe.

Unknown to scholarship until 2003 when it was rediscovered on the art market, and first published by the leading Flaxman authority David Bindman in *Apollo Magazine* in 2005, the relief has already generated a great deal of interest having been exhibited in Oxford at the Ashmolean; Berlin in a dedicated exhibition at the Bode Museum and London at Tate Britain.[1] The design had long been known from drawings in the British Museum and Yale Center for British Art and a plaster cast of the original model in the collection of the Sir John Soane's Museum, London, but these studies gave no sense of the finished marble, which because of its extraordinary quality and startling

individuality, Bindman has concluded was one of the very few sculptures Flaxman finished entirely himself, without studio assistance.[2] Despite the subject-matter being religious, the tender and intimate character of the design suggests that it was a highly personal work, possibly made for Flaxman's wife, rather than as a commission. This note offers a brief adumbration of the artistic and cultural context of the production of Flaxman's relief as well as its known history.

Flaxman, Neo-classicism and early Italian art

Flaxman arrived in Italy with his wife in 1787 at a highly important moment in the development of European taste. Connoisseurs, collectors and other artists were beginning to notice and explore early Italian art, discerning in works of the fourteenth and fifteenth centuries new and appealing qualities.[3] Flaxman's own early Italian notebooks are filled with observations on monuments not on the conventional itinerary of most Grand Tourists, which tended to focus on antiquities and works from the High Renaissance and Baroque. Flaxman was particularly attracted to *quattrocento* sculpture and painting. Whilst in Florence in November 1787, Flaxman recorded seeing a fresco by the fifteenth-century painter Lorenzo di Credi of *The Assumption of the Virgin* on the exterior wall of the convent adjacent to S. Croce, observing: *this composition is simple & grand, the character innocent & beautiful & the folds of the draperies marked with intelligence.*[4]

For Flaxman the simplicity and grandeur of early Italian sculpture and painting became a highly important influence on his own style.

These were qualities Flaxman had already encountered and explored in Etruscan vase painting. Before his departure for the Continent, Flaxman had been employed by Josiah Wedgwood to translate designs from ancient vases onto Wedgwood's ceramics. Flaxman had relied upon drawings of Etruscan vases in the collection of Sir William Hamilton, the British Minister in Naples, prepared by the Baron d'Hancarville.[5] The Etruscan designs disseminated by Hamilton, d'Hancarville and Wilhelm Tischbein had a demonstrable impact upon Flaxman's work. Scholars have long appreciated the economy of line and frieze-like arrangement Flaxman took from the vases, particularly in his pioneering illustrations to Homer and Dante.[6] Flaxman's trip to Italy was partially funded by Wedgwood and once in Rome he initially followed a conventional round of study, making a number of drawings from antiquities. His Roman sculptures reflect this initial interest and he produced a number of.compositions, most famously the *Fury of Athamas* for Frederick Hervey, 4th Earl of Bristol, which synthesised elements of the most noted Roman sculpture with subjects from antiquity. The *Fury of Athamas* relied for its composition on the ancient figure of *Niobe* in the Uffizi and *Laocoon* in the Vatican.

Whereas the *Fury of Athamas* recalls the sophistication of Canova's most heroic figure groups, the *Adoration of the Magi* is an altogether more solemn work that invokes quite deliberately the world of *quattrocento* painting, then in the process of being rediscovered. Flaxman arrived at a moment when Italian and resident European scholars, painters and collectors were beginning to explore and find new admiration for medieval art and antiquities.[7] One Englishman in particular was important in promoting interest in early Italian painting: the artist Thomas Patch, who lived in Florence from 1755 until his death in 1782.[8] In 1770 Patch published a

life of Masaccio with illustrations of frescos from the Brancacci Chapel in Florence and he habitually took British Grand Tourists to see the Chapel itself.[9] Patch was also a pioneering dealer, selling early Florentine paintings to travellers.[10] Perhaps most significantly, Patch was responsible for dispatching back to the newly founded Royal Academy casts of Ghiberti's *Gates of Paradise* from the Baptistery in Florence. Flaxman, who studied at the Royal Academy Schools in the 1770s, would undoubtedly have known the casts and shortly after arriving in Florence made a study from Ghiberti's doors themselves.[11]

But Patch's enthusiasm for early Italian art was inflected by his understanding of later sixteenth and seventeenth century works. In his life of Masaccio he included engravings of heads from Filippino Lippi's frescos in the Brancacci Chapel and his appreciation of Ghiberti was limited to the later, more decorated *Gates of Paradise* rather than the earlier north doors. Flaxman by contrast examined the New Testament scenes on the northern doors, making a series of studies in a sketchbook now at the Yale Center for British Art. As Hugh Brigstocke has pointed out, these drawings: 'focus on the low relief narrative but tend to ignore the physical context of each scene and to exclude naturalistic details in the immediate background.'[12] A fact Flaxman later reinforced in his Lecture 'On Composition', delivered at the Royal Academy in his capacity as Professor of Sculpture, 'it must be remembered, the work is sculpture, which allows no picturesque additions or effect of background; the story must be told, and the field occupied by the figure and acts of man.'[13] It was undoubtedly the clarity of action, stripped of all 'picturesque details', which stimulated Flaxman's attraction to early Italian sculpture and paintings. For the rest of his Italian trip, he sought out great works of

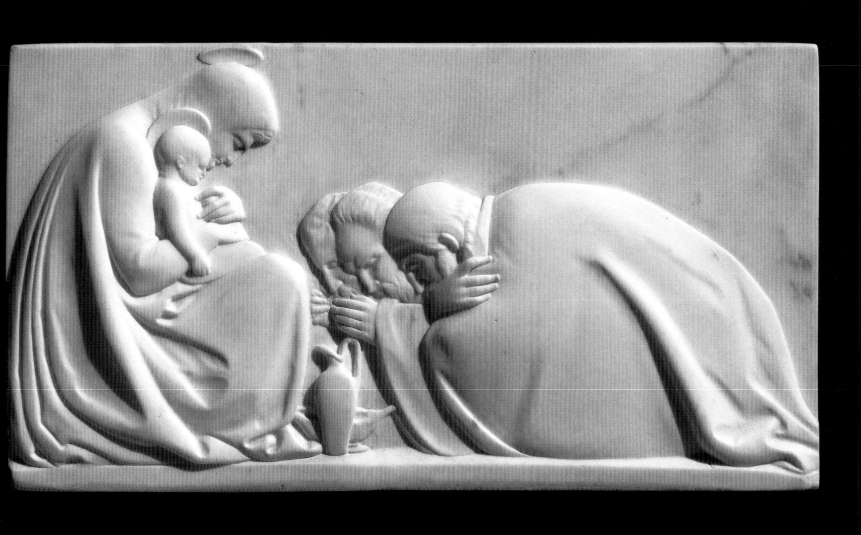

the *trecento* and *quattrocento*: his sketchbooks show he studied Cavallini's mosaics in S. Maria in Trastevere; in 1791 he copied two relief panels by Donatello and Ghiberti from the great font in the Baptistery at Siena; in 1794 he copied two panels, *The Agony in the Garden* and *Christ Returning to the Apostles*, from Duccio's *Maestà*, a thirteenth century work which had long been neglected by scholars and artists.

Flaxman's activity was in part inspired by meeting the young traveller William Young Ottley in 1792. Ottley, the scion of a wealthy merchant family, was an avid collector and draughtsman. He was employed in Rome by the French antiquarian Jean Baptiste Séroux d'Agincourt to make drawings for his illustrated survey of monuments, the *Histoire de l'Art par les Monuments depuis sa decadence au 4me Siècle jusqu' à son renouvellement au 16me Siècle*. In the process Ottley formed a

John Flaxman
The Nativity, from Ghiberti's Baptistery Doors, Florence
Italian sketchbook, studies from Florence and Rome, begun 1787
Pencil, pen and black ink and grey wash
8⅝ × 6 inches · 219 × 152 mm
Yale Center for British Art, Paul Mellon Collection, New Haven

large and impressive collection of studies of early Italian painting which he eventually published as: *A Series of Plates engraved after the Paintings and Sculptures of the Most Eminent Masters of the Early Florentine School* in 1826. Ottley rapidly became a firm friend of the Flaxmans, Mrs Flaxman recording their numerous meetings in her Italian journal.[14] There was a great deal of artistic and creative exchange between the two artists and it seems clear that they fostered in each other a love of early Italian art. Ottley copied two of Flaxman's drawings from the Yale sketchbook of Ghiberti's relief panels from the Baptistery doors, retaining them in his own collection. It was possibly through Ottley that Flaxman became acquainted with the Italian engraver Séroux d'Agincourt was employing to make plates for his work, Tommaso Piroli. Piroli would in turn be responsible for Flaxman's great series of line engravings from Homer and Dante.

Flaxman therefore has a very real claim for being at the forefront of the rediscovery of the Italian 'Primitives'. His Italian sketchbooks are full of drawings of Roman and medieval sculptures, but he was confirmed in his interest in early Italian art by the commission he received from Thomas Hope in 1792 for a series of illustrations to Dante's *Divine Comedy*. These caused him to look particularly at what he believed to be the art of Dante's time, at the *trecento* as well as the *quattrocento*. He studied almost all the major masters of both centuries available to him in both cities – 'the venerable sages who restored Philosophy and the Arts of Design' – and he also travelled to Orvieto, where he drew from Signorelli and Maitani. But despite Flaxman's fascination with early Italian painting, his sensitive appreciation of the qualities of 'simplicity', 'grandeur' and 'intelligence' he found in the works he saw, his role in the revival of interest in early Italian art has been constantly down-played, largely because very few of his surviving

works could be read as consciously 'primitive'. Whilst scholars such as David Irwin have identified echoes of early Italian painting in his engravings – particularly the series of illustrations to Dante – they are difficult to trace in his sculpture.[15] This makes the rediscovery of the *Adoration of the Magi* a highly significant, paradigm shifting one for the history of European neo-classicism.

The Adoration of the Magi

The small relief of the *Adoration of the Magi* – only 9 × 17 inches – is the embodiment of those artistic characteristics he sought in early Italian art. The massive cloaks of both Virgin and Magi are the most distinctive feature of the relief; by concealing and negating the body beneath, they deny the Greek heritage that is so conspicuous a feature of Flaxman's other Italian work. They evoke more than anything the monumental gravity of Masaccio's frescoes, which are themselves notably sculptural in their forms, and Ghiberti's handling of New Testament subjects from the northern Baptistery doors. Flaxman recorded his admiration for the group that contained what David Bindman has suggested was the closest precedent for his relief, Jacopo della Quercia's bas-relief of the same subject on the west facade of San Petronio in Bologna.[16] The Virgin and Child are also close to figures in Flaxman's drawings for *The Divine Comedy*, most notably for the figures of *The Child Cacciaguida* held by his mother in the illustration to *Paradiso*, Canto 15.

The composition precisely embodies those qualities which Flaxman most admired in early Italian painting; it is deceptively simple, intensely focused on the narrative at hand and stripped of all extraneous detail. The three Magi are shown kneeling, the bulk of their forms expressed simply by the body of the nearest Magus, the other two seen only in the receding profile of their heads. The Virgin is seated on the ground, her head bowed and covered, the folds of her drapery framing the small figure of the Christ child. The only ornament is a small ewer placed between the kneeling Magi and the Holy group. Flaxman carved the relief in shallow relief – although eschewing the formula pioneered by Dontatello, where incised lines are used to add greater recession – instead the bowed head of the Virgin, and deep vertical clefts of the Virgin's drapery and first Magus providing the areas of greatest contrast.

The precise circumstances for the production of the *Adoration of the Magi* are unknown. An unusually large number of studies survive for the relief, along with a cast and the preparatory sketch, there are several large-scale record drawings, all pointing to the significance of the piece to Flaxman himself. There are two large and highly finished drawings attributed to Flaxman in the British Museum and Yale Center for British Art which have provenances going back to the Flaxman family sale. There are uncertainties of draughtsmanship in both, particularly in the relationship between the second Magus's hand and the face of the Magus beyond that suggest they are in fact made by an artist other than Flaxman, perhaps from the marble or from a plaster version. In the Yale drawing the area around the third Magus's face has not been attempted at all, making it highly likely that it is in fact a studio work. These drawings are certainly more laboured and less accomplished than a smaller British Museum drawing. This sheet contains two vignettes. At the top is a scene from the story of Joseph and at the bottom the *Adoration of the Magi*. Although it seems likely to be the earliest drawing of the subject, it still retains a hesitancy in its execution which suggests it is in fact a copy drawing rather than a preparatory study.

John Flaxman
The Dream of Joseph and The Adoration of the Magi, 1792–4
Pen and grey ink with grey wash
7⅝ × 6¼ inches · 195 × 159 mm
© The Trustees of the British Museum

John Flaxman
The Adoration of the Magi, 1792–4
Grey wash · 10¾ × 18⅝ inches · 272 × 472 mm
© The Trustees of the British Museum

John Flaxman
The Adoration of the Magi, a design for bas relief, 1794
Pencil, grey wash and watercolour
11⅛ × 18 inches · 283 × 457 mm
Yale Center for British Art, Paul Mellon Collection, New Haven

John Flaxman
The Adoration of the Magi
Plaster cast
By courtesy of the Trustees of Sir John Soane's
Museum, London

It is frustrating that as yet we know
nothing for certain about the original
circumstances of the work, and cannot say
for certain whether it was carved in Italy or
London, although it certainly owes everything to Flaxman's Italian experience. It was
possibly made for someone close to him, and
Bindman has suggested that it might have
been made for his wife, Nancy, for whom
he often made special works, such as the
illuminated story *The Knight of the Blazing
Cross*. There are also records of other small
marbles he made in Italy, such as the 'little
medallion' sold to Thomas Hope and now
lost, and described by Mrs Flaxman as of
'about 6 Inches in the Diameter-of Dirce
sitting under a Vine & nursing the Infant
Bacchus--this is beautiful to the greatest
degree & finish'd like a Gem, it is admired
by all & desired by many But Mr Hope is the
fortunate Purchaser'. The value Flaxman
placed on the *Adoration of the Magi* as a
composition is confirmed by the survival
of at least two contemporary plaster casts
of the original clay model, made by Joseph
Denman, Flaxman's brother-in-law and long-
time studio assistant. The surviving versions
were included in the quantity of casts of
Flaxman's models acquired by Sir John Soane
from Maria Denman in 1834 and those given
to University College London in 1848.

Although the marble version at present
stands alone, there are indications that
Flaxman may have intended the design to

William Young Ottley
Portrait sketch of John Flaxman modelling a relief
Grey wash, brown ink and black chalk over pencil
3¾ × 2⅞ inches · 94 × 74 mm
© The Trustees of the British Museum

be part of what proved to be an abortive sequence of reliefs depicting the life of Christ. There are two other New Testament designs that can be considered with it: *The Flight into Egypt* and *The Three Marys at the Sepulchre* both now at University College London, and there is a possibility that plaster versions of the three compositions could have constituted the three 'sketch[es] in Bas Relief from the New Testament' exhibited at the Royal Academy in 1797.[17] Certainly, Flaxman did on other occasions put together a series of religious compositions. He produced finished drawings for *The Acts of Mercy* and *The Lord's Prayer*, clearly with the intention, not realised in his lifetime, of publishing them in an engraved form, but also using them as a quarry of ideas for single funerary monuments.

As Bindman has noted: '[t]he rarity of autograph marbles by Flaxman makes the recent reappearance of another one a notable event'. More than this, as this note has articulated, it is a highly personal and intimate piece, which deserves not only a place as one of Flaxman's most important works in marble, but as one of the most sophisticated and extraordinary sculptures of the late eighteenth century.

NOTES

1 See particularly: David Bindman, 'John Flaxman's Adoration of the Magi Rediscovered', *Apollo*, 162, no.526, 2005, pp.40-45 and Sylvie Tritz and Hans-Ulrich Kessler, *John Flaxman und die Renaissance; Ein Meister des Klassizismus im Dialog Masaccio und Donatello*, Skulpturensammlung und Museum für Byzantaninische Kunst Staatliche Museen zu Berlin, 2009.

2 David Bindman, 'John Flaxman's Adoration of the Magi Rediscovered', *Apollo*, 162, no.526, 2005, p.40.

3 The classic study of the revival of interest in early Italian painting remains Giovanni Previtali's *La fortuna dei primitivi dal Vasari al Neoclassici*, Rome, 1964.

4 Flaxman's Italian journal in the Fitzwilliam Museum, Cambridge, f.18r, reproduced in: eds. Hugh Brigstocke, Eckart Marchand and A.E. Wright, 'John Flaxman and William Young Ottley in Italy', *Walpole Society*, 2010, 72, p.98.

5 Eds. Ian Jenkins and Kim Sloan, *Vases and Volcanoes: Sir William Hamilton and his Collections*, Exh. Cat. London (British Museum), 1996, cat. no's, 60–61.

6 David Irwin, *English Neoclassical Art: Studies in Inspiration and Taste*, London, 1966, p.61.

7 F. Russell, 'Early Italian pictures and some English Collectors', *The Burlington Magazine*, vol. 136, no.1091, 1994, pp.85–90.

8 For Patch see: Edward Andrew Maser, 'Giotto, Masaccio, Ghiberti and Thomas Patch', in ed. Wolfgang Hartmann, *Festchrift Klaus Lankheit zum 20. Mai 1973*, Cologne, pp.192–199.

9 Patch's illustrations are in fact of heads from Filippino Lippi's frescos in the chapel, not Masaccio, but they were much discussed by collectors and painters during the century. In January 1771 Horace Walpole wrote to Horace Mann, the books dedicatee: 'It is the volume of Masaccio's designs, brought by Mr Coxe, I am transported with them! They are nature itself, and evidently the precursors of Raphael. He plainly availed himself of their dignity but scarce reached the infinite truth of their expression … I did not remember these works. Oh! If there are more, make your Patch give us all … I am expecting Sir Joshua Reynolds, our best painter, whom I have sent for to see … these heads of Masaccio. I think they may give him such lights as may raise him prodigiously.' Ed. Wilmarth Lewis, *The Yale Edition of Horace Walpole's Correspondence*, New Haven and London, 23, pp.266–7.

10 Fragments of Spinello Aretino's frescos from the destroyed Manetti chapel in Santa Maria del Carmine were purchased from Patch by Charles Townley as by Giotto in Florence in 1772. The fragments had been salvaged by Patch after a fire in 1771, they were purchased, according to Townley's account book for 48 scudi in February 1772. The frescos passed to William Young Ottley and were sold at Christie's, 25.iv.1811 (28) eventually passing to William Roscoe and are now in the Walker Art Gallery, Liverpool.

11 For Flaxman's studies of the Ghiberti doors see: eds. Hugh Brigstocke, Eckart Marchand and A.E. Wright, 'John Flaxman and William Young Ottley in Italy', *Walpole Society*, 72, pp.91–92, 122–24.

12 Hugh Brigstocke, 'Flaxman: Refocusing the Grand Tour', in eds. Hugh Brigstocke, Eckart Marchand and A.E. Wright, 'John Flaxman and William Young Ottley in Italy', *Walpole Society*, 2010, 72, p.6.

13 John Flaxman, *Lectures on Sculpture*, London, 1829, p.176.

14 For Ottley in Italy see: Hugh Brigstocke, 'William Young Ottley in Italy', in eds. Hugh Brigstocke, Eckart Marchand and A.E. Wright, 'John Flaxman and William Young Ottley in Italy', *Walpole Society*, 2010, 72, pp.341–359.

15 David Irwin, *John Flaxman, 1755-1826: Sculptor, Illustrator and Designer*, London, 1979, pp.94–106.

16 David Bindman, 'John Flaxman's Adoration of the Magi Rediscovered', *Apollo*, 162, no.526, 2005, p.43.

17 Algernon Graves, *The Royal Academy of Arts: A Complete Dictionary of Contributors and their work from its foundation in 1769 to 1904*, London, 1905, III, no.1106–1108, p.128.

LUCIUS GAHAGAN 1773–1855 (ATTRIBUTED TO)

Hugh Percy, 3rd Duke of Northumberland

Polychromed terracotta
Height · 24⅜ inches · 620 mm
Executed *circa* 1820–25

COLLECTIONS
Private collection, UK, 1958;
H Blairman & Sons;
Sir Gawaine and Lady Baillie, purchased
from the above, 15 July 1958, (described as
the Duke of Kent, 1815);
And by descent, 2013

This remarkable polychromed terracotta portrait is an unusual addition to the *corpus* of early nineteenth century British sculpture. This portrait has previously been identified as the Duke of Kent, the fourth son of George III and the father of Queen Victoria, albeit in a slightly idealized vein, however, recent research can now positively identify the sitter as Hugh Percy, 3rd Duke of Northumberland. It is evident that the present model was utilized by the Newcastle sculptors Christopher Tate and R. G. Davies for their full-length statue of the duke of *c.*1841 executed for the Master Mariners' Asylum at Tynemouth for which the Duke had given the site, and a large quantity of the materials employed in its construction.

The present work appears to be earlier than the commission which was entrusted to Christopher Tate of Newcastle-on-Tyne and completed on his premature death by his master R.G. Davies. A date in the first half of the 1820s would seem to stand based on historical and stylistic grounds and this is supported by the age of the sitter shown in our full-length portrait. Arrangements for the coronation of George IV in 1821 represented the apogee of the extravagance of the monarchy and provided a timely focus for the increasing taste for historicism and there was no greater outlet for this than the coronation and the ensuing procession and banquet in which the Duke of Northumberland played a prominent part wearing a fanciful Peers costume invented on antiquarian grounds for the ceremonies. Our terracotta portrait depicts the duke in a costume even more extravagantly 'historical' that has parallels with that seen in Christina Robertson's portrait.

Christopher Tate (1812–41) and R. G. Davies
(*fl.* 1820–57), *Hugh Percy, 3rd Duke of Northumberland*
Marble
Completed *c.*1841
Master Mariner's Asylum, Tynemouth

Richard Lane, after Christina Robertson
Hugh Percy, 3rd Duke of Northumberland
Lithograph, *c.*1825
13¾ × 10⅜ inches · 350 × 264 mm
© National Portrait Gallery, London

Lucius Gahagan
Richard Beadon, 1823
Plaster · height 9¼ inches · 235 mm
© National Portrait Gallery, London

An attribution to Lucius Gahagan (1773–1855) seems probable on stylistic grounds. Gahagan appears to have been an adaptable sculptor working in marble, wax and plaster and his commissions included funerary monuments as well as small full-length statues including that of George III, known in bronze (Royal Collection) and plaster (Royal Collection and Rose collection) as well as in a painted plaster version of 1818 (National Gallery of Victoria, Melbourne). The present work can be compared with Gahagan's statuette of Richard Beadon, Bishop of Bath and Wells which is known in patinated plaster casts (National Portrait Gallery and another version) which demonstrates a similar handling especially in the elements of the drapery and passementerie. Lucius appears to have worked closely with his brother Sebastian who was responsible in 1824 for a full-length stature of the Duke of Kent (Park Crescent, Portland Place, London) and there also appears to be some confusion also as to whether the smaller works attributed to his father, Lawrence Gahagan (c.1735–1820) should be given to Lucius. The most cogent account of Gahagan's elusive career can be found in Ingrid Roscoe's *Biographical Dictionary of Sculptors in Britain*.

The Duke, a Tory, sat in in the House of Commons before succeeding to the Dukedom in 1817. Charles Greville thought the duke: 'a very good sort of man, with a very narrow understanding, an eternal talker, and a prodigious bore', and Northumberland's views were to become increasingly illiberal with the years.[1] The duke's prodigious wealth and fondness for magnificence did, however, have its uses to George IV, a monarch who appreciated the importance of outward display, and in 1825 was appointed as Ambassador Extraordinary at the coronation of Charles X of France, defraying the expenses himself whilst he 'astonished the continental nobility of the magnitude of his retinue, the gorgeousness of his equippage, and the profuseness of his liberality'. Four years later his Ambassadorial paraphernalia came in handy when he was appointed Lord-Lieutenant of Ireland with instructions to give Dublin a semi-regal performance: a caravan carrying £90,000 worth of the duke's plate from the Paris mission was seen passing through Staffordshire on its way to Dublin, escorted by a body of soldiers. Some contemporaries found it a surprising appointment, considering the duke's political inexperience, and his reputation as 'a stupid, prosing, man' and 'an amazing bore', and his strong anti-Catholic views. Nevertheless it was, in Peel's view, an inspired choice: when Northumberland resigned along with the Wellington government in November 1830 he described him as 'the best chief Governor who ever presided over her [Ireland's] affairs.'[2]

NOTES

1 Ed. Henry Reeve, *The Greville Memoirs, A Journal of the Reigns of King George IV, King William IV and Queen Victoria*, London, 1899, I, p.164.
2 N. Gash, *Mr Secretary Peel: the life of Sir Robert Peel to 1830*, London, 1961, p.654.

DANIEL GARDNER 1750–1805

Lady Elizabeth Townsend

Pastel and gouache
20 × 15¾ inches · 510 × 400 mm · oval
In the original neo-classical, frame
Executed in 1776

COLLECTIONS
The sitter;
Harriet Townsend, daughter of the above,
who married Sir Grey Skipwith, 8th Bt.;
Sir Grey Skipwith, 11th Bt., to c.1920;
Mrs J. M. Dennis, 1954;
J. Leger & Son, London;
Mrs Gore Skipwith, acquired from the
above, 1955;
Private collection, UK, 2013.

LITERATURE
Neil Jeffares, *Dictionary of Pastellists before
1800*, London, 2006, p.191.

Daniel Gardner's portraiture occupies an unusual position within the history of British painting during the eighteenth century. By the late 1770s, Gardner was one of the most successful and prolific painters in London having created a hugely popular portrait formula; reproducing in pastel on small-scale the fashionable poses and conceits of full-sized works by Sir Joshua Reynolds and George Romney. Conversely, unlike the masters he imitated, Gardner's success was achieved without the use of London's exhibiting societies: he showed only one picture at the Royal Academy and never submitted a work to the Society of Artists. As a result Gardner has received comparatively little scholarly attention, although the range, importance and number of his sitters suggests that he was a significant member of the wider artistic community and his beautifully executed and engaging portraits are a fascinating

testament to the success and adaptability of 'Grand Manner' portraiture.[1] All these elements are visible in this hugely accomplished and finely handled portrait of Lady Elizabeth Townsend.

Gardner was born in Kendal in Cumbria and after leaving school worked with George Romney. Romney left Kendal for London in 1762, and Gardner followed in either 1767 or 1768, living initially at 11 Cockspur Street, very close to the Royal Academy Schools in Pall Mall which he joined in 1770.[2] On leaving the schools, Gardner joined Joshua Reynolds's studio as an assistant in exchange for further tuition. Gardner was therefore working for Reynolds at the moment he was experimenting with his grandest and most impressive exhibition portraits. Shortly after establishing his own practice, Gardner began to produce works in pastel which closely followed the fashions established by his former master, simply replicating poses and compositions on a more domestic scale. The present portrait, which depicts Lady Elizabeth Townsend, the daughter of Other Lewis Windsor, 4th Earl of Plymouth, was probably made on the occasion of her marriage in 1776 to Gore Townsend, perfectly illustrates Gardner's working method. Lady Elizabeth Townsend is shown standing, in loose classical costume, in a wooded landscape in a pose which is directly modelled on Reynolds's full-length portrait of *Georgiana, Duchess of Devonshire*, which was exhibited at the Royal Academy in 1776 and is now in the Huntington Art Collections, San Marino, California. Gardner adapted Reynolds's pose slightly, placing a rose in the right-hand of Lady Elizabeth Townsend, but otherwise he precisely replicated the costume, setting and attitude.

Gardner developed a novel technique using pastel to approximate the appearance of oil. By combining pure pastel with a liquid vehicle he was able to create a range of textures, from the soft rendering of features and hair, to the more broadly handled landscape.[3] In the present work the areas of greatest opacity, such as Lady Elizabeth Townsend's costume, are all created using Gardner's distinctive technique. The domestic scale of Gardner's works, their charm and sweetness meant he was frequently commissioned to paint family groups and children. The present work is an extremely fine example of Gardner's technique and manner, perfectly illustrating why he was such a successful artist. It was Gardner's clever distillation of Reynolds and Romney's style into a domestic scale which made him so popular with French and American collectors of the early twentieth century.

NOTES
1 Gardner was the subject of an exhibition at Kenwood House: Helen Kapp, *Daniel Gardner 1750–1805*, exh.cat. London (Kenwoood House), 1972 and a book: George Williamson, *Daniel Gardner*, London, 1921. But comparatively little has been written about him subsequently and he is omitted from standard accounts of eighteenth-century British art.
2 Helen Kapp, *Daniel Gardner 1750–1805*, exh.cat. London (Kenwoood House), 1972, unpaginated introduction.
3 Neil Jeffares, *Dictionary of Pastellists before 1800*, London, 2006, p.191.

HUGH DOUGLAS HAMILTON 1739–1808

Charles, Lord Lecale (1756–1819)

Pastel over pencil
9 × 7 inches · 230 × 190 mm
Drawn *circa* 1779

COLLECTIONS
William FitzGerald, 2nd Duke of Leinster,
the sitter's brother;
Augustus FitzGerald, 3rd Duke of Leinster
when recorded at Carton House, Kildare,
in 1885;
By descent, 2013.

LITERATURE
Catalogue of Pictures and Antiquities at Carton,
1885, pp.33–35, no.4.
Neil Jeffares, *Dictionary of pastellists before
1800* (online edition).

This characteristic pastel portrait by the
Irish artist Hugh Douglas Hamilton depicts
Charles FitzGerald, third son of James
FitzGerald, 1st Duke of Leinster and his
wife Lady Emily Lennox. Emily Lennox was
a daughter of Charles Lennox, 2nd Duke of
Richmond and great-granddaughter of King
Charles II. Her sisters contracted a series of
famous (and infamous) marriages resulting in a complex but close family network
which stretched from Ireland to London.
The present portrait of Charles, a naval
officer, who would be created Lord Lecale
in his own right in 1800, and that of his first
cousin, the Whig politician Charles James
Fox (see p.55), were part of a remarkable
group of pictures depicting members of
the extended Leinster and Lennox families
which decorated two of the greatest houses
of eighteenth-century Ireland, Carton
House and Castletown.[1] In exceptionally
good preservation, the present unpublished portrait is a charming example of

Hamilton's work and belongs to perhaps his
most extensive and significant commission.

Hugh Douglas Hamilton was born in
Dublin, the son of a wig maker in Crow
Street. He entered the Dublin Society School
of Drawing about 1750 and studied under
Robert West and James Mannin. He was a
pupil there for some eight years, winning
three premiums for the best drawings of
1756. His earliest recorded work for the
FitzGerald family came in 1760, when he
illustrated the frontispiece of the estate
atlas of Kilkea, a manor owned by James
FitzGerald, later 1st Duke of Leinster.[2]
Hamilton probably left West's academy in
the late 1750s and soon set up a flourishing
business as a portraitist in pastels.

Hamilton's small-scale, intimate pastel
portraits were immensely popular. Their
popularity rested on a combination of the
luminous surface quality he achieved, the
speed of execution (unlike oils, pastels
required no drying time), portability and low
cost. As a result of their popularity in 1764
Hamilton moved his practice to London,
although he continued to preserve strong
contacts with his native Ireland, returning
periodically and sending works for exhibition
at the Society of Artists in Dublin.

It was their comparatively inexpensive-
ness which was the most important factor in
their popularity. Hamilton's average price for
a small oval portrait was 9 guineas according
to his earliest biographer Thomas Mulvany.[3]
Compared with prices being charged by
leading London portraitists for oil portraits

Hugh Douglas Hamilton
*Self-portrait, c.*1791
Pastel and pencil · 8⅞ × 6¾ inches · 225 × 170 mm
Photo © National Gallery of Ireland
NGI.19554

(Joshua Reynolds was commanding up to 50 guineas for a half-length work during the 1770s), Hamilton's pictures offered an expeditious way of having a large number of smaller likenesses of friends and family in a single room. Portraiture was a traditional way of expressing loyalties whether dynastic, political or ones of friendship. At Carton House the 2nd Duke of Leinster brought together a series of thirty-six portraits by Hamilton of his siblings and cousins.[4] According to a later inventory twenty-eight of these pastels were in an oval format and arranged in the 'Duke's Study', the present portrait of his brother Charles, Lord Lecale was listed as no.4.[5]

Like many younger sons, Charles entered the Navy at a young age, being commissioned a lieutenant in 1777. He was given his first command, *HMS Tapegeur*, in 1779 and it seems likely that Hamilton's portrait commemorates this event. Hamilton left for Italy the same year, although he resumed work for the Duke of Leinster on his return in 1790s completing a series of pastel portraits of him and his wife. Charles had an illustrious naval career, participating in the Battle of Chesapeake in 1781, a decisive French victory during the American War of Independence, before retiring with the rank of Rear-Admiral in 1790 and being made Lord Lecale in 1800.

NOTES

1   As Ruth Kenny noted: 'by far the most regular and long-standing patrons of his work in pastel was the extended Conolly-Leinster family.' Ruth Kenny, 'Blown from the face-powders of the age'; the early pastel portraits *c.*1760–1780', in ed. Anne Hodge, *Hugh Douglas Hamilton: A life in Pictures*, exh.cat. Dublin (National Gallery of Ireland), 2008, p.21.

2   Anne Crookshank and the Knight of Glin, *The Watercolours of Ireland*, London, 1994, p.66.

3   Thomas James Mulvany, 'Memoirs of Native Artists: Hugh Douglas Hamilton', *Dublin Monthly Magazine*, January 1842, p.69.

4   For the number of pastels see: Ruth Kenny, 'Blown from the face-powders of the age'; the early pastel portraits *c.*1760–1780', in ed. Anne Hodge, *Hugh Douglas Hamilton: A life in Pictures*, exh.cat. Dublin (National Gallery of Ireland), 2008, p.21.

5   *Catalogue of Pictures and Antiquities at Carton*, 1885, pp.33–35.

Hugh Douglas Hamilton
William Robert Fitzgerald, later 2nd Duke of Leinster (1749–1804), *c.*1773
Pastel and pencil · 8 × 6⅜ inches · 202 × 162mm
Photo © National Gallery of Ireland
NGI.3022

HUGH DOUGLAS HAMILTON 1739–1808

The Right Hon. Charles James Fox (1794–1806)

Pastel over pencil
9 × 7 inches · 230 × 190 mm
Drawn *circa* 1777

COLLECTIONS
William FitzGerald, 2nd Duke of Leinster,
the sitter's first cousin;
By descent to Augustus FitzGerald, 3rd Duke
of Leinster, by descent recorded at Carton
House, Kildare in 1885;
By descent until 2013.

LITERATURE
Catalogue of Pictures and Antiquities at Carton,
1885, pp.33–35, no.16.
John Ingamells, *The National Portrait Gallery:
Mid-Georgian Portraits 1760–1790*, London,
2004, p.166.[1]
Neil Jeffares, *Dictionary of pastellists before
1800* (online edition).

This finely rendered and highly sensitive
portrait of the Whig politician Charles
James Fox was drawn by the Irish portraitist, Hugh Douglas Hamilton for William
FitzGerald, 2nd Duke of Leinster. Fox and
Leinster were first cousins, their mothers
having been two of the notorious Lennox
sisters, daughters of Charles Lennox, 2nd
Duke of Richmond and granddaughters of
King Charles II. The present pastel was one
of a series of thirty-six commissioned by the
Duke of Leinster to decorate a room at his
Irish seat, Carton House. The survival of
this previously unpublished work offers fascinating evidence of pastel portraits and their
use in commemorating personal and familial
ties during the eighteenth century. More
than this, as a very fine, highly sensitive and

Carton House, co. Kildare

private portrait of one of the most famous figures of the eighteenth century it is an important addition to both Hamilton's *oeuvre* and Fox's iconography.

Probably made in 1777 on one of Fox's visits to Ireland, it was commissioned by his first-cousin William FitzGerald, 2nd Duke of Leinster. As Ruth Kenny has recently explained, Hamilton's small-scale pastel portraits: 'functioned as personal documents, reinforcing familial and social ties in an affectionate rather than in a genealogical way … they operated on a network rather than lineal system and built up a more complex, layered picture of a family and its social life than any single work could achieve.'[2] This idea of the personal network the Duke of Leinster created is confirmed by a nineteenth-century inventory of the pictures of Carton House, which lists some thirty-six pastels in the 'Duke's Study'. It is an idea given added weight by the survival of a series of copies of the Carton Hamiltons. A version of the present portrait of Fox survives at Castletown, the home of another of Leinster's first-cousins, Thomas Conolly.[3] Leinster in turn had a version of Hamilton's portrait of Conolly, thus reinforcing the strong ties between the two families.[4]

Simply portrayed, bust-length, against a monochrome background, Hamilton's portrait of Fox eliminates all extraneous details and props. Unlike the more celebrated portraits of Fox, such as Reynolds's half-length portrait of 1782 (Holkham Hall, Norfolk), which shows him with his hand resting on a draft of the India Bill, Hamilton's depiction concentrates on Fox's animated features. Finely finished in Hamilton's characteristic manner, the present picture is an extraordinary testament to the ties of family which governed eighteenth century Britain.

Hugh Douglas Hamilton
The Right Hon. Charles James Fox
Pastel · 9 × 7½ inches · 230 × 190 mm
© The Castletown Foundation,
courtesy of The Office of Public Works

NOTES

1 It is unclear whether the present work is the portrait mentioned by Ingamells as being in a 'private collection', or whether it is the portrait currently belonging to the Castletown Foundation.

2 Ruth Kenny, 'Blown from the face-powders of the age': the early pastel portrait, *c*.1760–1780', in ed.Anne Hodges, *Hugh Douglas Hamilton (1740–1808); A Life in Pictures*, exh.cat., Dublin (National Gallery of Ireland), 2008, p.21.

3 Reproduced in ed. Anne Hodge, *Hugh Douglas Hamilton: A life in Pictures*, exh.cat. Dublin (National Gallery of Ireland), 2008, cat.no.26.

4 Conolly's portrait is reproduced in ed. Anne Hodge, *Hugh Douglas Hamilton: A life in Pictures*, exh.cat. Dublin (National Gallery of Ireland), 2008, cat.no.14. For the Leinster version of the portrait see: Neil Jeffares, *Dictionary of Pastellists before 1800*, online edition.

VICTOR-MARIE HUGO 1802–1885

Landscape

Pen and brown ink and wash,
with gum arabic
1½ × 4⅜ inches · 38 × 112 mm
Signed and dated, lower left, *Victor Hugo. 1842*

COLLECTIONS
Ian Woodner, 1990;
Dian Woodner and Andrea Woodner,
by descent to 1993;
Private collection, New York, 2012.

ENGRAVED
Etched by Louis Marvy, 1847

Théophile Gautier, the writer and critic,
observed in June 1837:
Victor Hugo is not only a poet, he is also a
painter and one whom Louis Boulanger; Camille
Roqueplan or Paul Huet would not disavow as
a father … if he were not a poet, Victor Hugo
would be a painter of the first rank … He excels
in mixing in his sombre and wild fantasies
the chiaroscuro of a Goya with the terrifying
architectural effects of a Piranesi.[1]

Victor Hugo, the great French Romantic
poet, novelist, and playwright, although best
known today for his novels was in addition
to his abundant literary output a prolific
draughtsman, producing over 2,000 drawings
during his lifetime. As opposed to his written
work, published to great critical acclaim and
known by a wide contemporary audience,
Hugo generally considered his drawings
as a private activity, created for his own
pleasure and enjoyment, and not intended
for public consumption although they
achieved considerable fame amongst artistic
circles in his lifetime. Despite Gautier's
public praise, most were unaware of Hugo's
drawings during his lifetime, as he never
exhibited them publicly. The present work
is a comparatively early and extraordinarily

intense example, perfectly capturing the
confluence of Goyesque-chiaroscuro and
terrifying architecture of Piranesi, first noted
by Gautier.

The first exhibition of Hugo's drawings
took place in Paris in 1888. Greater aware-
ness has come with subsequent exhibitions
in the 1970s and 1980s. The great majority of
Hugo's drawings are today in the Maison de
Victor Hugo in Paris and in the Bibliothèque
Nationale, Paris. Hugo's drawings fall
loosely into several different categories – the
early caricatures; the naturalistic landscapes
of the 1840s; the fantasy, or imaginary, landscapes of the 1840s and 1850s, often showing castles and towers; and the loose and
abstract works, including ink-blots (*taches*),
of the 1850s and 1860s.[2] The present sheet,
simply entitled, *Landscape*, is a relatively
early and naturalistic work, signed and dated
by Hugo, 1842. It depicts a real landscape,
probably somewhere around Paris, where
the artist was living at the time, developed
into a Romantic fantasy.

In his 1837 essay, Gautier observed
that: 'when he travels [Hugo] he sketches
everything that strikes him. The ridge of a
hill, a broken-line, a strangely formed cloud,
a curious detail on a door or window, a
ruinous tower, an old belfry , these things
he notes; then at evening, in the inn, he
inks in his pencil sketch, puts in shadows
and colouring, strengthens it, brings out an
effect that is always boldly selected.' This
explication of Hugo's working method
gives a vivid idea of the combination of
direct observation and emotional response
to the landscape discernible in the present
drawing. The richness in the application
of ink and its skilled and assured handling
are reminiscent of the landscape drawings

of Rembrandt, whilst the areas of velvety
texture and calligraphic lines suggest Hugo's
interest in etchings. The importance of our
sheet to Hugo is evident in that it was one
of four drawings he gave five years later,
in 1847, to the engraver, Louis Marvy, in
order for Marvy to make etchings of the
subjects to be used as prizes in a lottery. An
etching of 1847 after the present sheet, in
reverse and also entitled, *Landscape*, is in the
Bibliothèque Nationale, Paris.[3] In technique
– the summary yet confident execution – the
present drawing places Hugo firmly within
the orbit of other French Romantic painters
of the period, particularly Paul Huet, whom
Gautier had observed, would not 'disavow'
Hugo as a father. Indeed, Delacroix was to
observe that if Hugo had decided to become
a painter instead of a writer, he would have
outshone the artists of their century.

NOTES
1 T. Gautier, ed and trans. F. C. Sumichrist, *The*
   Works of Théophile, New York, 1908, 23, p.152–3.
2 See Paris, Musée du Petit Palais, *Soleil d'Encre:*
   Manuscrits et Dessins de Victor Hugo, exhibition
   catalogue, 3 October 1985 – 5 January 1986,
   p.95, figs. 107a, 107b, illustrated.
3 For Hugo's work of the 1840s, see: F. Rodari *et*
   al., Shadows of a Hand: The Drawings of Victor
   Hugo, exhibition catalogue, New York, The
   Drawing Center, 16 April – 13 June 1998, p.14,
   fig. 7, illustrated.

SIR THOMAS LAWRENCE PRA 1769–1830

Arthur Atherley

Oil on canvas
24½ × 20 inches · 622 × 508 mm
Painted in 1791

COLLECTIONS
Andrew Coventry, acquired in Edinburgh
in 1860;
By family descent, to 2013.

LITERATURE
Kenneth Garlick, 'A Catalogue of the paint-
ings, drawings and pastels of Sir Thomas
Lawrence', *The Walpole Society*, 1962–64, vol.
39, p.24;
Michael Levey, *Sir Thomas Lawrence*, exh.cat.
London (National Portrait Gallery), 1979,
p.29;
Kenneth Garlick, *Sir Thomas Lawrence:
A complete catalogue of the oil paintings*, 1989,
p.141, under catalogue no.50.

Sir Thomas Lawrence PRA
Arthur Atherley, 1792
Oil on canvas · 62⅜ × 52⅜ inches · 1584 × 1330 mm
Los Angeles County Museum of Art, California,
Gift of Hearst Magazine

This exceptional painting was made by
Thomas Lawrence in preparation for his early
masterpiece *Arthur Atherley* (Los Angeles
County Museum of Art). Lawrence exhibited
his painting of *Atherley* at the Royal Academy
in 1792 at a key moment in his early career
and it marked his transition from precocious youth to mature master. The present
preliminary study shows how determinedly
Lawrence pursued this path. The sketch –
showing Atherley in a blue coat, rather than
the distinctive red one which features in the
final portrait – is a remarkably assured essay,
both in virtuosic technique and penetrating
characterisation. In the boldly direct pose,
starkly lit from one side, Lawrence created
one of the most intense portraits of the late
eighteenth century. In the present sketch this
is amplified by the spare use of paint and
unfinished quality, which isolates and focus
attention on the head. Last on the market in
1860, the present painting has remained in the
same family and has never previously been
exhibited, reproduced or fully published. As
such it is an immensely important addition to
Lawrence's *oeuvre*, shedding new light on his
working practice at the outset of his career.[1]

Thomas Lawrence was the outstanding
British portraitist of the first quarter of the
nineteenth century, the third President of
the Royal Academy and a hugely influential
European master, whose paintings had a
profound impact upon Continental portraiture.[2] Born in Bristol in 1769, the son of an
excise officer, he was celebrated as a child
prodigy, producing pastel portraits first in
Devizes and then Bath, before moving to
London in 1787. After studying at the Royal
Academy Schools, Lawrence rapidly established himself as artistic heir to Reynolds,
exhibiting 12 portraits at the Academy in 1790,

including celebrated full-length depictions of
Queen Charlotte (National Gallery, London)
and the actress *Elizabeth Farren* (Metropolitan
Museum, New York).[3] The following year
he was elected an Associate of the Royal
Academy, at the age of only 22.

At some point in 1791 Lawrence began his
painting of Arthur Atherley. Atherley was
the son of a Southampton based banker, also
called Arthur, and was in his last year at Eton
College.[4] Whilst the provenance of the Los
Angeles painting suggests it was a family
commission – it descended in the Atherley
family until acquired by Joseph Duveen on
behalf of William Randolph Hearst in 1928 –
Lawrence clearly saw it as an opportunity to
consolidate his public successes on the walls
of the Royal Academy at the annual exhibition. This was a prospect given an added
boost by the death of Reynolds in February
1792, which resulted in the position of Painter
in Ordinary to the King falling vacant. As
a plan of the hang at the exhibition of the
Royal Academy, made by Thomas Sandby,
shows, *Atherley* was well placed on the west
wall of the Great Room at Somerset House,
slightly to the left of one of the main doors.
Lawrence therefore transformed the commission into a major statement of his artistic
abilities, at a crucial moment in his career.
It was a project that would have demanded
multiple sittings, and even multiple canvases,
as the appearance of the present painting
demonstrates.

In 1790 Lawrence observed that: 'I should
think it is always better that the picture,
whatever it is, be first accurately drawn on
the canvas.' We know from contemporary
accounts that this was the case. In 1794 Joseph
Farington recorded: 'this morning I sat to
Lawrence when He drew in my portrait with

Thomas Gainsborough RA
Jonathan Buttall 'The Blue Boy', c.1770
Oil on canvas · 70 × 44⅛ inches · 1778 × 1121 mm
© Courtesy of the Huntington Art Collections,
San Marino, California

black chalk on the Canvass, which employed him near 2 Hours. He did not use colour today.'[5] Lawrence seems to have used liquid, light brown paint to work out Atherely's pose, traces of which can be faintly seen in the lower sections of the canvas. Lawrence normally used a canvas with a white or off-white ground, precisely as he has done in his portrait of Atherley. In providing advice on painting in 1790 to the amateur artist Lady Malden, he explained: 'I always endeavour to paint a picture as light as possible even at first colouring', adding, 'Now when an artist endeavours to paint bright at first, the next time he comes he will try to make it still more and so on, till by this struggle with himself he will at last gain a degree of brilliancy as unexpected as it must be gratifying …'[6] During the second sitting

Lawrence would colour the face, bringing it more or less up to completion, before working on the background and costume in subsequent sessions. The present canvas was designed as a bust-length portrait and has only been slightly reduced in size along the top-edge, suggesting that Lawrence intended the picture to be more or less the current format, and therefore not the same size as the finished picture. This demands the question of the status of the current work, is it a second version or the first sketch?

The unfinished status of the present work is probably explained by Lawrence's desire to preserve the character and life-like quality captured in his first sittings. Lawrence's earliest biographer Andrew Cunningham, noted in 1833: 'Lawrence sometimes, nay often, laid aside the first drawing and painted on a

copy.'[7] For 'drawing' in this case we should read 'painting' – in his use of liquid colour to suggest the costume and pose, Lawrence was literally drawing with the brush – making the present painting the first study from which he completed the Los Angeles canvas (the 'copy'). The status of this painting as the first sketch is substantiated by comparison with the finished portrait. In the Los Angeles painting Atherley's features are subtly different in their handling and execution: his face has been lengthened, his nose given greater definition, his eyes widened and hair made more glossy and voluminous. All this contributes to the sense that Atherley is slightly older in the Los Angeles version. Throughout the composition, the particularities of the present oil study have been replaced by bold generalisations in the finished canvas. This is precisely the process Lawrence would undertake in preparation for a major work for the walls of the Academy, where verisimilitude could be sacrificed to overall effect.

Several accounts of the Academy exhibition identified the sitter as Thomas Sheridan, the precocious son of the playwright Richard Brinsley Sheridan, rather than Atherley, confirming the ambiguity inherent in contemporary portraiture where stylisation was the norm.[8] In the finished painting it is clear to see that the sitter has become a vehicle for Lawrence's virtuosic handling of paint: dressed in a striking red jacket, slashed through with the white of his waistcoat and set against a brooding landscape with Eton College chapel in the distance. The present study has none of these theatrical elements. It is instead a penetrating portrait study of Atherley stripped of any of the conventional portrait painters' props and theatricality.

Rather than a red coat, Lawrence originally dressed Atherley in blue. This last detail may be explained by what we

Receipt from D. Bruce & Co., Edinburgh, Edinburgh, 3 July 1860

know of Lawrence's understanding of colour and his great desire to triumph on the overcrowded walls of the Academy. In 1828 John Burnet published his *Practical Treatise on Painting*, in which the author praised Thomas Gainsborough's portrait of *Gainsborough Dupont*(?), then known as the 'Blue Boy' and now in The Huntington, for disproving Reynolds's rule that cool colours (blue, grey or green) should never predominate in a composition.[9] Lawrence wrote to Burnet disagreeing with him, observing that: 'I should instance for one the ascendancy of white objects, which can never be departed from with impunity, and again the union of colour with light. Masterly as the execution of that picture is, I always feel a never-changing impression on my eye that the Blue Boy of Gainsborough is a difficulty boldly combated not conquered.'[10] Lawrence would have known Gainsborough's portrait of about 1770 well – it was auctioned in 1796 and again in 1802, when it was acquired by the portraitist John Hoppner – he was possibly even consciously emulating it in his portrait of Atherley.[11] It is highly suggestive that by 1860, when the present painting was sold in Edinburgh, the surviving receipt identifies it as: 'the first sketch of the Blue Boy by Gainsborough.'

The three-quarter length Los Angeles painting marks Atherley leaving school, attaining majority and entering adulthood. It would be natural to find multiple versions (given to family members, tutors etc.), but the present sketch seems to be the only other related painting and as a sketch occupied a vastly different and more important position from that of replica or copy. The present painting possibly remained in Lawrence's studio until his death, although it is not identifiable amongst the hundreds of canvases sold at his posthumous sale in 1830. As a preliminary study, the present painting preserves an intensity, vitality and freshness absent in the finished canvas; it is

characteristic of Lawrence's virtuosic technique at a crucial moment of his career as well as being the highly engaging first study of one of his most celebrated paintings.

NOTES

1 Whilst the present picture was listed by Garlick in 1962 and 1989, until the present catalogue it had never been professionally photographed or published.

2 For Lawrence's impact on French painting see: Ed. Patrick Noon, *Crossing the Chanel: British and French Painting in the Age of Romanticism*, exh.cat., London (Tate Gallery), 2003.

3 For Lawrence's early career see: Michael Levey, *Sir Thomas Lawrence*, New Haven and London, 2005, pp.25–65.

4 For a discussion of the Huntington portrait, see: Michael Levey, *Sir Thomas Lawrence*, exh. cat. London (National Portrait Gallery), 1979, cat.no.6; eds. Cassandra Albinson, Peter Funnell and Lucy Peltz, *Thomas Lawrence: Regency Power & Brilliance*, exh.cat. London, (National Portrait Gallery), 2011, cat.no.5.

5 Ed. Kenneth Garlick and Angus Macintyre, *The Diary of Joseph Farington*, New Haven and London, 1, p.187.

6 London, Royal Academy Archive, LAW / ⅟32. Draft letter from Sir Thomas Lawrence to Viscount Malden, July 1790.

7 Allan Cunnigham, *The Lives of the Most Eminent British Painters*, London, 1833, 6., p.195.

8 Kenneth Garlick, *Sir Thomas Lawrence: A complete catalogue of the oil paintings*, 1989, p.141.

9 John Burnet, *Practical Hints on Colour in Painting*, London, 1828, p.2. Recent research has challenged the traditional identity of the sitter as Jonathan Buttall to Gainsborough's nephew, Gainsborough Dupont. See: Susan Sloman, 'Gainsborough's *Blue Boy*,' *The Burlington Magazine*, 155, April 2013, pp.231–237.

10 Lawrence's comments were published in John Burnet's edited edition of Reynolds's *Discourses*. Ed. John Burnet, *The Discourses of Sir Joshua Reynolds, Illustrated by Explanatory Notes & Plates by John Burnet, F.R.S.*, London, 1842, p.155.

11 For the history of Gainsborough's portrait, see: Robyn Asleson and Shelley M. Bennett, *British Paintings at the Huntington*, New Haven and London, 2001, cat.no.17, pp.104–111.

SIR THOMAS LAWRENCE PRA 1769–1830

Charles James Fox

Oil on canvas
30 × 25 inches · 763 × 635 mm
Painted in 1800

COLLECTIONS

Major-General, the Hon. George Walpole
(1758–1835), painted for him at St Anne's Hill,
Chertsey, November 1800;
Henry Richard Vassall-Fox, 3rd Baron
Holland, (1773–1840) a gift from the above;
Lady Mary Elizabeth Fox, daughter of the
above (Lady Mary Elizabeth Lilford (née
Fox) become the sole heiress of the Holland
family in 1859);
Thomas Powys, 3rd Lord Lilford, husband of
the above, d.1861;
Thomas Littleton Powys, 4th Lord Lilford.
d.1896;
John Powys, 5th Lord Lilford, d.1945;
Stephen Powys, 6th Lord Lilford, d.1949;
George Vernon Powys, 7th Lord Lilford,
to 1961;
Sidney F. Sabin, acquired from the above
in 1961;
Private collection, 2013.

LITERATURE:

George Otto Trevelyan, *Life and Times of Lord
Macaulay*, London, 1888, p.153;
Earl of Ilchester, *The Home of the Hollands*,
London, 1937, p.139;
Kenneth Garlick, *Sir Thomas Lawrence*,
London, 1954, p.37;
Kenneth Garlick, *Sir Thomas Lawrence PRA,
1769 – 1830*, exhibition catalogue, 1961, cat.
no.36;
Kenneth Garlick, 'A Catalogue of the
Paintings, Drawings and Pastels of Sir Thomas
Lawrence', *The Walpole Society*, 1964, 39, p.81;
Kenneth Garlick and A. Macintyre (ed.),
The Diary of Joseph Farington, New Haven and
London, IV, p.1450;
Kenneth Garlick, *Sir Thomas Lawrence;
a complete catalogue of the oil paintings*, Oxford,
1989, cat.no.307;
John Ingamells, *National Portrait Gallery
Mid-Georgian Portraits, 1760–1790*, London, 2004,
p.168 reproduced.

EXHIBITED

London, Royal Academy, *Sir Thomas Lawrence
PRA, 1769–1830*, 1961, no.36.

Horace Hone after Lawrence
Charles James Fox
Enamel on copper · 1¾ inches high
Signed, inscribed and dated 1807
Lowell Libson Ltd

*His features, in themselves, dark, harsh, and
saturnine, like Charles II, derived a sort
of majesty from the addition of two black and
shaggy eyebrows, which sometimes concealed, but
more frequently developed, the workings of his
mind … His figure, broad, heavy, and inclined
to corpulency, appeared destitute of elegance or
grace, except the portion conferred on it by the
emanations of intellect.*

Sir Nathaniel Wraxall, 1815[1]

The great Whig politician Charles James
Fox was one of the most frequently depicted
figures of the second-half of the eighteenth
century; his features – 'dark, harsh and
saturnine' – being familiar from countless
paintings, miniatures, busts and satirical
cartoons. For over thirty years Fox's politics
pursued an increasingly radical ideology,
supporting American independence and the
power of parliament over King George III,
as such he became a cult figure not only in
aristocratic Whig circles, but to democratic
campaigners across the world. Fox's image
was therefore mass produced and widely
disseminated, but never was he as sensitively
or compellingly portrayed as by Thomas
Lawrence in the present little-known
picture. Painted in 1800, this portrait is the
last great painting of Fox before his death
in 1806.[2] Although a concentrated study,
the lively touch and insightful depiction of
character confirm that this work belongs to
Lawrence's period of masterly productivity
which would culminate in the celebrated
series of portraits made after the victory of
the Napoleonic Wars. It is rare that a portrait
combines so recognisable a sitter with a
painter of such celebrity and yet because of
its descent in various private collections has
remained virtually unknown having only

been exhibited once, at the Royal Academy in 1961.

Charles James Fox belonged to a grand Whig family and early in his political life he became a prominent and staunch opponent of George III, whom he regarded as an aspiring tyrant; he supported the American Patriots, even dressing in the colours of George Washington's army. Briefly serving as Britain's first Foreign Secretary in the ministry of the Marquess of Rockingham in 1782, he returned to the post in a coalition with his old enemy Lord North in 1783. However, the King forced Fox and North out of government before the end of the year, replacing them with the twenty-four-year-old William Pitt and Fox spent the following twenty-two years facing Pitt and the government benches from across the Commons. In 1797, after the suspension of *Habeas Corpus* and the extension of the law of treason and the ignominious defeat of Fox's motion for peace with France, the Foxite minority withdrew from Parliament. In 1799 Fox was struck off the Privy Council for proposing a toast to the people.[3]

The political situation and his own unconventional personal life meant that from 1797 Fox spent most of his time at St Ann's Hill, Chertsey. St Ann's Hill had been purchased in 1785 from the Duke of Marlborough by Elizabeth Armistead, a former courtesan, who had become Fox's wife in 1795. The couple kept their marriage secret until 1802. Their evidently happy domestic life is reported by the gem engraver Nathaniel Marchant and recorded in the diary of the landscape painter Joseph Farington: *Their manner of living is, to breakfast at 9, – dine at 4, Coffee and Tea soon after 6, then walk, then Cards, a slight Supper at 9, and to bed at 10.*

Their table plain – A little girl a daughr. of Mr Fox, but not by Mrs Armistead was there[4]

It was at this moment of political defeat that the 'cult of Fox' emerged. In 1802 the sculptor Joseph Nollekens produced his most celebrated bust of Fox, showing him without a wig, wearing the short hair of the Roman late Republic, and austerely without costume. This, the most enduring and replicated depiction of Fox, was so popular that by 1807 Farington reported that Nollekens had already produced twenty-one versions of the bust and had commissions for a further eight.[5] One version in particular points to the immense importance of Fox's image to the Whig party at the turn of the nineteenth century. In 1802 Francis Russell, 5th Duke of Bedford constructed at Woburn Abbey a 'Temple of Liberty' to house Nollekens's bust of Fox.[6] The temple, designed by Henry Holland, also contained busts of Fox's political allies and friends – Earl Grey, Earl Spencer, Lord Holland, James Hare and General Fitzpatrick – and on the exterior housed antique busts of the great Roman Republicans, Lucius Junius Brutus and his son Marcus Junius Brutus. As Nicholas Penny has noted 'the temple was an act of symbolic support, an elaborate gesture of solidarity, made by the Foxite minority in their darkest hour.'[7]

All the same ingredients evident in the Woburn Temple of Liberty arguably come together in Lawrence's portrait of Fox which, significantly dates from two years earlier. It was Farington again who records Lawrence's visit to Fox in Surrey and the sittings for the present portrait. On 4 November 1800, he noted: *Lawrence & Smirke dined with me … Lawrence has been at St. Anns Hill & painted portrait of Fox.*

Joseph Nollekens (1737–1823)
Charles James Fox
Marble · height 26½ inches · 673 mm
© National Portrait Gallery, London

John Jones, after Sir Joshua Reynolds
The Rt Hon Charles James Fox, 1784
Mezzotint · 20 × 14 inches · 510 × 359 mm
© The Trustees of the British Museum

– surprising simplicity of Character in his domestic capacity.[8]

The simple bust-length portrait, which was presumably executed in one or two sittings, is surprising in its economy, sensitivity of handling and intensity.[9] Lawrence eliminated all colour in the costume and background, save for the luminous and thickly painted white stock and orange waistcoat. Instead the portrait is a concentrated essay in Fox's features; his glistening eyes and hugely expressive eyebrows, which, as Wraxall noted, 'developed, the workings of his mind.' This austerity is in marked contrast to earlier portraits of Fox, such as Reynolds's three-quarter length portrait at Holkham, which shows him in a grand Baroque setting, his hand resting on a draft of the India Bill.[10] Lawrence's Fox, as in Nollekens's bust of 1802, is shown with his own hair cut short, in the manner of Roman Republican portrait busts and significantly contemporary Revolutionary France. This radical departure may have been a piece of conscious self-fashioning, as at this date, Fox was calling himself the 'English Brutus' in his correspondence.[11] Fox felt that he had been defeated by the rising tyranny of Pitt who he saw as the new Augustus, a feeling Lawrence communicated in his portrait by showing him stoically isolated, with a look of resignation. The present picture therefore anticipates the more overt expressions of the 'cult of Fox' celebrated in the Temple of Liberty at Woburn.

Lawrence's portrait also commemorates the political friendship which was so central to the 'cult of Fox'. The painting was commissioned not by the heavily indebted Fox, but by Major General George Walpole, a Whig MP who served as Under-Secretary of State for Foreign Affairs, when Fox was Foreign Secretary in 1806. Walpole was a devoted Foxite and presented Lawrence's portrait to Fox's heir and nephew, Henry Richard Vassall-Fox, 3rd Baron Holland. Lawrence's portrait therefore fits precisely into the same context as Nollekens's busts: it commemorates Fox in the mode of a Roman Republican standing up to tyranny and was commissioned by a friend and political ally. As with the Nollekens bust there is evidence that Lawrence was asked to paint replicas. His bank ledgers reveal that he was paid for a copy by Edward Bouverie, an old school friend of Fox's, in 1806.[12] There was also a copy of the portrait included in Lawrence's studio sale listed as being by his assistant and pupil John Simpson.[13]

This little known portrait by Lawrence is perhaps the most expressive, sympathetic and powerful images of Fox. In his virtuosic and fluid use of paint, Lawrence imparts a remarkable sense of humanity to the politician's features. Given the present painting's date, its format and provenance, it demands to be reconsidered as not only as important evidence in Fox's careful fashioning of his image after 1800, but as one of the finest portraits of the sitter ever executed.

NOTES

1   Sir Nathaniel Wraxall, *Historical Memoirs of my own time*, London, 1815, II, p.224.

2   Although a number of later pictures of Fox survive – including a full-length portrait by John Opie now at Holkham Hall which was exhibited at the Royal Academy in 1804 – none have the gravity or power of earlier works. For the iconography of Fox see: John Ingamells, *National Portrait Gallery Mid-Georgian Portraits, 1760-1790*, London, 2004, pp.163–169.

3   Leslie Mitchell, *Charles James Fox*, Oxford, 1992.

4   ed. K. Garlick and A. Macintyre, *The Diary of Joseph Farington*, New Haven and London, I, p.235.

5   ed. K. Garlick and A. Macintyre, *The Diary of Joseph Farington*, New Haven and London, VIII, p.3060.

6   John Kenworthy-Browne, The Temple of Liberty at Woburn Abbey', Apollo, CXXX, July 1989, pp.27–32.

7   Nicholas Penny, 'The Whig Cult of Fox in Early Nineteenth-Century Sculpture', *Past & Present*, 70, February 1976, p.98.

8   ed. K. Garlick and A. Macintyre, *The Diary of Joseph Farington*, New Haven and London, IV, p.1450.

9   The posthumous sale of the contents of Lawrence's studio includes two 'studies for the Head of C. Fox on canvas'. These may have been the initial studies made at St Ann's Hill in November 1800. Christie's, 18 June 1831, lot 13.

10 David Mannings and Martin Postle, *Sir Joshua Reynolds: A Complete Catalogue of his Paintings*, New Haven and London, 2000, no.674.

11 Leslie Mitchell, *The Whig World*, London, 2005, p.28.

12 This version is recorded by Garlick as a copy of the present work. See Kenneth Garlick, *Sir Thomas Lawrence; a complete catalogue of the oil paintings*, Oxford, 1989, cat.no.307. This version was incorrectly identified as the primary version in: Geoffrey Ashton, *Sir Thomas Lawrence*, London, 2006, pp.70–71.

13 Christie's, 18 June, 1831, lot. 79.

EDWARD LEAR 1812–1888
The Cedars of Lebanon

Pencil, pen and ink and watercolour
14¾ × 21¼ inches · 375 × 540 mm
Inscribed, dated and numbered:
The Cedars / Lebanon / 20 . 21 May 1858 (193)

COLLECTIONS
Franklin Lushington, from the artist
by gift or purchase;
Sir John Witt;
and by descent to 2013

LITERATURE
Vivien Noakes, *Edward Lear*, 1979, repr.
opposite p.240;
Vivien Noakes, *Edward Lear 1812–1888*, exhibition catalogue, 1985, p.112 and reproduced in
colour p.70

EXHIBITED
London, Arts Council, *Edward Lear*, 1958,
no.34;
London, Gooden & Fox, *Edward Lear*, 1968,
no.66, (on loan);
London, The Fine Art Society, *The Travels
of Edward Lear*, 1983, no.86, (on loan);
London, Royal Academy of Arts, *Edward
Lear 1812–1888*, 1985, no.26

Lear arrived in Beirut from Jerusalem on
11 May 1858 and a few days later described in
letter to his sister his approach to the cedars:
*So fine a view I suppose can hardly be imag-
ined – more perhaps like one of Martin's ideal
pictures:- the whole upper part of the mountain
is bare & snowy, & forms an amphitheatre
of heights, round a multitude of ravines &
vallies – full of foliage & villages most glorious
to see: – and all that descends step by step to the
sea beyond! – Far below your feet, quite alone
on one side of this amphitheatre is a single dark
spot – a cluster of trees: these are the famous
Cedars of Lebanon.= Lebanon doubtless was
once thickly covered with such, but now there are
these only left. – I cannot tell you how delighted
I was with those cedars! – those enormous old
trees – a great dark grove – utterly silent, except
the singing of birds in numbers. Here I staid all
that day – the 20th & all the 21st working very
hard … only that there was a leettle drawback to
my pet cedars – & that was, that being 6000 feet
above the sea, & surrounded by high now peaks
the cold was o great I could not hold my pencil
well …* [1]

The cedars of Lebanon are generally
considered to be amongst the subjects that
inspired Lear to the greatest heights of
poetry and ambition in his paintings.
Indeed, Lear considered that the nine-foot
painting (now lost) of the cedars which
was based on the present 'on the spot'
study and additional recourse to a group
of cedars in the grounds of Oatlands Park
Hotel near Weybridge, to have been his
most important work. Lear worked on that
painting in the winter of 1860–61 after his
return to England and on its completion
exhibited it at the Royal Academy in 1862
with a price of 700 guineas. In spite of Lear's
regard for the picture it did not meet with
the reception he had hoped for and he was
to write to Chichester Fortescue in 1867,
the year in which it was purchased by Lady
Ashburton, that: 'Sometimes I consider as to
the wit of taking my cedars out of its frame
and putting it in the border of coloured
velvet, embellished with a fringe of yellow
worsted with black spots, to protypify the

Edward Lear, *The Cedars of Lebanon*
Oil on canvas · 26¾ × 44¾ inches · 68 × 113.5 cm
Painted for Charles Roundell
Courtesy of Peter Nahum at The Leicester Galleries,
London

The Cedars
Lebanon,
on 25 May 1858

(193)

possible proximate propinquity of predatorial panthers – and then selling the whole for floorcloth by auction.' The painting is now known through a smaller replica commissioned by Lear's friend Charles Roundell.

Vivien Noakes has pointed out that in choosing the cedars, Lear could combine the biblical association of the subject with a subject drawn from nature. This was especially important as Lear considered that his particular strength lay in the depiction of natural history and often referred to his 'poetical, & accurate topographical delineation', emphasising that the lifelike quality of his work was important to him. In a humorous reference to a painting of the Cedars, Lear wrote that the picture was: 'so advanced that millions of sparrows are said to sit – (I never saw them myself,) on the window ledges, pining with hopeless despair at not being able to get inside.'[2]

Franklin Lushington the first owner of this watercolour was the object of Lear's most fervent and most painful friendship. Lear first met the young barrister in 1849 in Malta where Franklin's elder brother Henry was Chief Secretary to the government and then toured southern Greece with him. Lear developed an undoubted passion for him that Lushington did not reciprocate. In 1855, he was appointed judge to the Supreme Court of Justice in the Ionian Islands, and Lear went with him to Corfu where he settled for some years. Although they remained friends for almost forty years until Lear's death the disparity of their feelings for one another constantly tormented Lear. On his death, Lear left all his papers to Lushington, who later destroyed most of them

The present sheet numbers amongst the masterpieces of Lear's large drawings made on tour. The subject evidently had great emotional resonance for him and the intricate and loving execution and level of finish lavished on the present sheet underlines that fact. Lear made another large 'on the spot' drawing of the cedars dated 21st May 1858 (Victoria & Albert Museum). A similarly sized carefully worked-up replica of the present watercolour which was made for a Miss Clive Perrystone of Ross-on-Wye and was on the London art market in 1996.[3]

NOTES

1 Letter to Ann Lear, 26th May 1858, Private collection.
2 Letter to Marianne North, 30 April 1861, Perkins Library, Duke University.
3 Christie's, July 9, 1996, lot 62, £91,700.

Edward Lear, *The Cedars of Lebanon*
Pen and Ink and Watercolour · 13¾ × 21½ inches
Inscribed and dated and numbered:
The Cedars, Lebanon. 21 May, 1858
© Victoria & Albert Museum

Watercolour with scratching out and gum arabic · 4⅝ × 7¼ inches · 117 × 184 mm
Signed with monogram
Painted *c.*1860

COLLECTIONS
Private collection, acquired in the 1960s

This carefully finished watercolour is one of the most beautiful examples of the small watercolours that Lear made, often on speculation on his return from his tours, with the intention that they could be purchased immediately from his studio rather than engaging in the often lengthy process of executing a commission. Sometimes these small pictures are unfairly regarded as inferior works on account of a comment of Lear's when he referred to them as his 'Tyrants' and, indeed, there are many small watercolours of inferior quality where one can understand Lear's frustration in being tied to his studio. This particularly beautiful view of the cedars numbers amongst the most careful and gem-like of his smaller works. Our watercolour dates from the early 1860s and uses the monogram form of his signature that he first adopted in late 1858.

This treatment of his favourite subject appears to be derived from the 'on the spot' study in the Victoria & Albert Museum.

WILLIAM MARLOW 1740–1813

Rome from the Tiber

Pencil and grey, blue and pink wash
13⅞ × 21 inches · 354 × 534 mm
Signed: *W Marlow* (lower left)
Drawn in the 1770s

COLLECTIONS
Christian B. Peper;
and by descent, 2012.

This fine drawing, showing the dome of St Peter's Basilica, the Castel Sant'Angelo and Ponte Sant'Angelo viewed from the Tiber, exemplifies Marlow's ability as a topographer as well as a being a fine example of Grand Tour draughtsmanship.

Marlow's early works, like those of Samuel Scott, his master, clearly show the influence of Canaletto who visited London in 1746. Marlow's early success is evinced by the painter Thomas Jones who recorded in his *Memoirs* for 1769 that when he was beginning his own career Marlow was one of the artists 'in full possession of the landscape business', and later the Royal Academician Edward Garvey recalled to Joseph Farington that when he had first arrived in London in the 1760s he found Richard Wilson and William Marlow especially successful, and that 'Marlow's work captivated him so much that … he thought that as a Young Man he would rather be Marlow than Wilson.'[1]

According to an obituary notice which appeared following his death in January 1813, Marlow: 'went on his travels to France and Italy in 1765 by the advice of the late Duchess of Northumberland.' His patron was Elizabeth Seymour-Percy, wife of Hugh Smythson, 1st Duke of Northumberland and one of Canaletto's great patrons, thus reaffirming Marlow's links with the Italian *vedute* painters of the previous century. A group of eight Italian paintings of Tivoli, Arriccia, and scenes in the Bay of Naples survive at Alnwick Castle confirming the duchess's sponsorship of his tour of France and Italy. The earliest note of his departure is found on a drawing of an English river scene inscribed 'William Marlow the Author of this Drawing is now studying in Italy – July 8th 1765'; the only other dated record of his absence occurs in Richard Hayward's list of artists in Rome in February 1766.[2] The itinerary he followed through France and Italy is well documented by drawings and paintings, including an album containing a series of Italian views now in the Tate.

The studies contained in the Tate album, formerly in the Oppé collection, formed the basis for a large number of works produced after his return from the Continent. It is highly likely that the present sheet is one such watercolour. A pen and ink drawing in the Tate album shows the identical composition, one which was extremely popular during the seventeenth and eighteenth centuries amongst Continental view painters. Taken from the west bank of the

William Marlow
Rome: Castle S. Angelo and St Peter's, c.1765
Pencil and ink · 8½ × 13¼ inches · 214 × 337mm
© Tate, London 2013

William Marlow
View of Rome from the Tiber, c.1775
Oil on canvas · 39¾ × 50⅛ inches · 1010 × 1273mm
Philadelphia Museum of Art,
Gift of Jay Cooke, 1955

Marlow was freed from the necessity of topographical accuracy, so dresses the view with fanciful trees on the left and figures in the foreground.

Marlow exhibited several views of Rome at both the Society of Artists and Royal Academy and in addition to the present watercolor there are four large scale oil paintings by Marlow of the same view, the most impressive of which is now in the Philadelphia Museum of Art. The enduring popularity of such compositions amongst English collectors enabled Marlow to move his studio from Leicester Fields to the manor house at Twickenham in 1775, where he died in 1813.

Tiber, somewhere between the Teatro di Tor di Nona and the Arco detto di Parma and showing three of the most renowned sights of the city – the Ponte Sant'Angelo topped with Bernini's sculpted angels, the three domes of St Peter's Basilica and the monumental brick, Castel Sant'Angelo – it was one of the most popular views of Rome drawn by amongst others Gaspar Vanvitelli, Giuseppe Zocchi, Bernardo Bellotto, Claude-Joseph Vernet and Giovanni Battista Piranesi. It was probably for precisely this reason, and as a favorite amongst collectors and travellers, that Marlow took such care in preparing the Tate study, which was designed to be used for finished watercolours back in London.

Indeed from 1766 Marlow largely specialized in producing watercolours and paintings of Continental subjects. He showed his first such pictures at the Society of Artists in 1767, and the great majority of his 134 paintings and watercolours exhibited with the Society of Artists, the Free Society of Artists, and the Royal Academy from then onwards were of French and Italian subjects together with London views which continued the Canaletto–Scott tradition. The present watercolour is a tonally subtle translation of the Tate sketch – the areas annotated on the Tate sheet with colour notes, such as 'dark' on the building to the far left correspond precisely to the present drawing – Marlow keeps colour to a minimum, instead modelling the view in washes of brown, grey and blue. Away from Rome

NOTES

1 Eds. Kenneth Garlick and Angus Macintyre, *The Diary of Joseph Farington*, New Haven and London, 1979, VI, p.2244.
2 Eds. Kenneth Garlick and Angus Macintyre, *The Diary of Joseph Farington*, New Haven and London, 1979, VI, p.2244.

SAMUEL PALMER 1805–1881

A rocky shore with distant sailing boats

Watercolour and gouache
11¼ × 16 inches · 286 × 406 mm
Painted c.1849

COLLECTIONS
A. H. Palmer, the painter's son;
The Richmond family;
Stephen Spector, New York;
Davis Galleries, New York;
Edwin P. Rome, acquired from the above,
1968;
And by descent, 2013

LITERATURE
Raymond Lister, *Catalogue raisonné of the works of Samuel Palmer*, 1988, no.485, repr.

EXHIBITED
New York, Davis Galleries, *19th century English Watercolors*, 1968, no.32.

In the years following his return to London from Shoreham, Palmer was constantly exploring the possibilities of what he could achieve in watercolour, his chosen medium; looking for an avenue by which he could be true to his artistic ideals whilst finding a commercial voice. From the mid-1830s Palmer repeatedly made studies of the sea and coastline many of which have been traditionally identified as having been executed on his occasional visits to North Devon. He was evidently fascinated by the dazzling effects of light on water as his small *plein air* studies demonstrate, and he frequently included the device of a setting sun on water in many of his major compositions.

Christina Payne has recently underlined Palmer's abiding interest in the connection between land and sea and has reconsidered Palmer's relationship with the marine painter James Clarke Hook.[1] Certainly, marine themes increasingly play an important part in the works of Palmer's middle years and especially so after the death of his eldest son.

This rare and highly worked watercolour is one of the most atmospheric treatments of a coastline by Palmer. The particular and intense treatment of the foreground may be compared with the drawing of *Waves breaking upon the seashore, Cornwall* (National Gallery of Canada, Ottawa) which, although executed in a different medium, demonstrates a similar response to the forms and textures shown in our work. In the present watercolour, tentatively identified as being at Margate on the basis of an old inscription on the verso of the drawing, Palmer has produced one of his most carefully worked exercises in which he treats the sky, the sea and the foreground shingle beach with loving and compelling intensity. Palmer explained his fascination thus:
Why, from childhood onwards, are we ever dreaming of capes and caves, and islets and headlands, and the marriage of the land and sea?[2]

This drawing was used by Lord David Cecil to illustrate his A.W. Mellon Lecture series at the National Gallery of Art, Washington, entitled 'Visionary and Dreamer, Two Poetic Painters: S. Palmer and E. Burne-Jones.' His lecture was later published and illustrated with a small selection of images of works in public collections.

Samuel Palmer
Sunrise over the sea
Watercolour over black and blue chalk heightened with bodycolour · 5¼ × 7 inches · 130 × 180mm
Private collection USA (formerly with Lowell Libson Ltd)

NOTES
1 Christina Payne, 'Dreaming of the marriage of the land and sea'; Samuel Palmer and the coast', in ed. Simon Shaw-Miller and Sam Smiles, *Samuel Palmer Revisited*, Farnham, 2010, pp.65–82.
2 Letter to James Clarke Hook, May 1863. See Ed. Raymond Lister, *The Letters of Samuel Palmer*, Oxford, 1974, II, p.680.

SIR JOSHUA REYNOLDS PRA 1723–1792

Macbeth: A first idea of the figure of Macbeth on seeing the witches

Pen and brown ink
9½ × 7½ inches · 241 × 192 mm
Inscribed on backing sheet: *By Sir Joshua Reynolds. First idea of the figure of Macbeth on seeing the witches.*
Drawn 1787

LITERATURE (for a discussion of the finished painting):
Martin Postle, *Sir Joshua Reynolds: The Subject Pictures*, Cambridge, 1995, p.267–272;
Renate Procho, *Joshua Reynolds*, Weinheim, 1990, p.195–7;
Henry Graves & William Cronin, *History of the Works of Sir Joshua Reynolds*, London, 1899–1901, vol. III, p.1172.

In 1787 Reynolds wrote to his friend and patron, Charles Manners, 4th Duke of Rutland:

The greatest news relating to virtu is Alderman Boydel's scheme of having pictures of the most interesting scenes of Shakespear, by which all the painters and engravers find engagements for eight or ten years; he wished me to do eight pictures, but I have engaged only for one. He has insisted on me taking earnest money, and to my great surprise left upon my table five hundred pounds – to have as much more as I shall demand.[1]

Boydell's Shakespeare Gallery was one of the most elaborate schemes for the promotion of contemporary art undertaken during the eighteenth century and given his celebrity, as the founding President of the Royal Academy and leading theoretician on painting, Reynolds's involvement was clearly crucial for its success. Reynolds chose as his 'one' canvas a subject from Macbeth, for which the present sheet is the first recorded study.

Contemporary newspapers reported that Reynolds had chosen 'The Pit of Acheron' as his subject, this was the setting of Act 4, Scene 1, in which Macbeth visits the witches to have confirmation of their prophecies and they summon horrid apparitions to allay his fears. Reynolds was clearly enthralled by the opportunity to depict the supernatural machinery introduced by Shakespeare: thunder, a cavern, witches round a cauldron conjuring apparitions at the demand of Macbeth. The scale of the canvas Reynolds

was given by Boydell, recorded in his Pocket Book as 'Cloth 8f. 6 high / 12 f. – long', combined with the prestige of the commission probably prompted Reynolds to produce a number of ink sketches of the composition before beginning the painting itself. A compositional study survives at the Beinecke Rare Book and Manuscript Library, Yale University showing Macbeth with the witches; the present previously unrecorded and unpublished study clearly precedes the Beinecke sheet being a preliminary idea for the figure of Macbeth, and must be considered the earliest surviving drawing for scheme.

In contrast to the finished painting, now at Petworth House, West Sussex, where Macbeth is shown from behind, clearly fearful of the witches apparitions, Reynolds originally planned him as a heroic Baroque general, right arm outstretched commandingly silencing the witches. The change in character from triumph to fear suggests the contemporary cultural shift in the reading of Shakespeare. Early in the century producers and critics had been unwilling to integrate the witches with the 'real' characters in the play. Consequently, they were presented separately from the main drama, as a *divertissement*, performing comic dances with broomsticks and singing songs. By the 1780s they were reinstated into the main drama and seen as integral participants. In painting this shift meant Macbeth was seen as offering episodes which perfectly

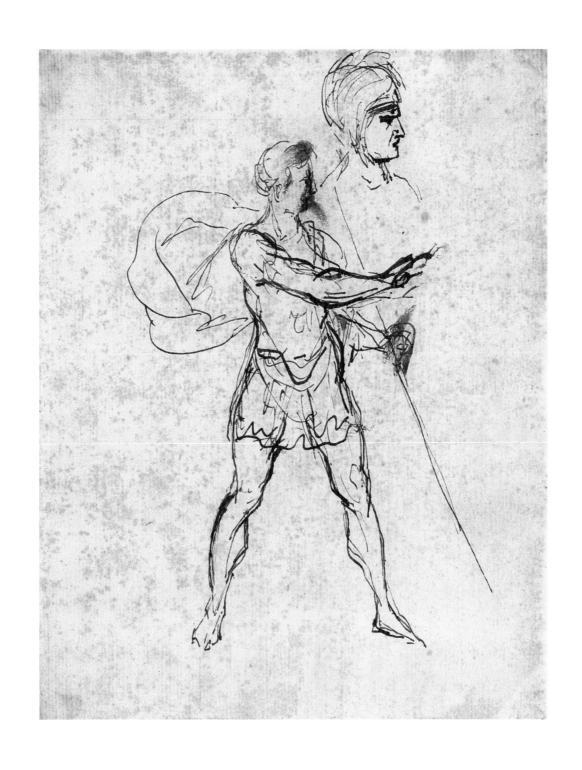

accorded with Edmund Burke's definition of the sublime. Painters such as Henry Fuseli, who specialised in capturing scenes of the supernatural, began to depict episodes from the play, including Act 4, Scene 1. Reynolds clearly saw the potential for depicting a savage landscape and all the supernatural paraphernalia of Shakespeare's text. For the figures he turned to a host of old master sources, including Michelangelo and in the pose of Macbeth, as it was realised in the final painting, according to J.M.W. Turner, Leonardo da Vinci's *Vitruvian Man*, although as Martin Postle has pointed out, he is closer to James Barry's *Satan* from his etching of *Satan Summoning up his Legions*. The final painting was the subject of a dispute between Reynolds and Boydell and remained in Reynolds's studio until his death in 1792 when it was sold, along with this study, at his studio sale. Today *Macbeth and the Witches* is wholly legible only in Robert Thew's 1802 engraving, the picture itself having darkened considerably over the past 200 years.

On a pen and ink study of *Hecate* (Private Collection), also made for *Macbeth*, there is an inscription, in the same hand as the present sheet, noting: 'Sir Joshua seldom made any sketches with a pencil, or pen, and when he did so, was usually very careful, to destroy them immediately; such sketches therefore and by chance have been preserved on account of their rarity.'[2]

This fluid and confident pen and ink study is an extremely rare example of a figure sketch directly related to one of Reynolds's most important historical compositions. In its strength, poise and drama it undermines Reynolds's reputation as a poor draughtsman.

NOTES
1 J. Reynolds, ed. F. W. Hilles, *The Letters of Sir Joshua Reynolds*, Cambridge, 1929, p.174.
2 This inscription is recorded in M. Postle, *Sir Joshua Reynolds: The Subject Pictures*, Cambridge, 1995, p.267.

Sir Joshua Reynolds
Macbeth and the Witches, 1788–90
Oil on canvas
Petworth House, West Sussex
© National Trust Images

Robert Thew, after Sir Joshua Reynolds
Macbeth and the Witches, 1802
Etching · 19⅝ × 24⅞ inches · 497 × 631 mm
© The Trustees of the British Museum

THOMAS ROWLANDSON 1756–1827

Etching and engraving by Robert Pollard (1755–1838) and aquatint by Francis Jukes (1747–1812)

Vauxhall Gardens

Etching, engraving and aquatint printed in warm brown ink on wove paper
21⅛ × 29⅝ inches · 535 × 753 mm
Published by John Raphael Smith,
28 June 1785

I remember the time when Vauxhall (in 1776, the price of admission being then only one shilling) was more like a bear garden than a rational place of resort, and most particularly on the Sunday mornings … Rowlandson the artist and myself have been there, and he has found plenty of employment for his pencil. The chef d'Oeuvre of his caricatures, which is still in print, is his drawing of Vauxhall, in which he has introduced a variety of characters known at the time.

> H. Angelo, *Reminiscences of Henry Angelo, with Memoirs of his Late Father and Friends*, London, 1830, ii, p.1.

The print of Thomas Rowlandson's *Vauxhall Gardens* is one of the graphic masterpieces of the eighteenth century.[1] It depicts the celebrated pleasure grounds in London populated by a mix of famous and infamous characters, from the Prince of Wales (later George IV) to the celebrated brothel-keeper Mrs Barry (the 'Old Bawd of Broad Street') and has become one of the quintessential images of recreation and urban life in London. The present impression is a remarkably rare extremely early impression which fully displays the depth of tone Francis Jukes was able to achieve with aquatint. The date, quality, beauty and outstanding condition of the present impression make it both a highly decorative and desirable print and a fascinating document of one of the eighteenth century's most distinct phenomena: the pleasure garden.

Vauxhall Gardens, on the south bank of the Thames, entertained Londoners and visitors to London for two hundred years.[2] From 1729, under the management of Jonathan Tyers, property developer, impresario and patron of the arts, the gardens grew into an extraordinary business, a cradle of modern painting – with supper boxes decorated with paintings by Francis Hayman and Hubert Gravelot in the 1730s – architecture, sculpture, and music. A pioneer of mass entertainment, Tyers had to become also a pioneer of mass catering, of outdoor lighting, of advertising, and of all the logistics involved in running one of the most complex and profitable business ventures of the eighteenth century in London.

By the 1750s the site comprised a series of tree-lined walks, pavilions in the latest Rococo taste (these included a Chinese Temple, Gothic Obelisk and Turkish Tent) and large provision of supper rooms for dining and a rotunda seventy feet in diameter for indoor performances. The gardens attracted large numbers of Londoners – in 1749 a rehearsal of Handel's *Music for the Royal Fireworks*, was attended by 12,000 people – from a cross-section of London society. Frederick, Prince of Wales was an early patron, along with many leading fashionable celebrities and musical performers, many of whom gave concerts in the gardens. Most importantly the modest entrance fee – as Angelo noted only a shilling – made it accessible to London's burgeoning middle and artisanal classes. The diarist James Boswell observed of Vauxhall's appeal: [*It] is peculiarly adapted to the taste of the English nation; there being a mixture of curious show, — gay exhibition, musick, vocal and instrumental, not too refined for the general ear; — for all of which only a shilling is paid; and, though last, not least, good eating and drinking for those who choose to purchase that regale.*[3]

It is not surprising, therefore, that Rowlandson should have been a frequent visitor and, to quote Angelo again, found there: 'plenty of employment for his

Drawn by T. Rowlandson.　　　　　Aquatinta by F. Jukes.　　　　　Engraved by R. Pollard.

VAUX-HALL.

London Published June 28.th 1785 by J.R. Smith No. 83 Oxford Street.

pencil.' Whilst Rowlandson's sense of the absurd is Hogarthian, his fluid, confident drawing style owes much to French art. Rowlandson's aunt and financial supporter was of Huguenot extraction and he made a number of visits to France throughout the 1770s where he was exposed to not only French draughtsmen, but Continental subjects, which resulted in several early masterpieces, such as the *Place des Victoires* (Yale Center for British Art).

In 1783 Rowlandson exhibited three works at the Royal Academy, one was simply entitled *Vaux-Hall*. This was almost certainly the watercolour now in the Victoria and Albert Museum on which the present print is based and which was praised in the contemporary London press for being: 'conspicuous for genuine humour.'[4] The composition depicts a view of the Grove at Vauxhall from the Rotunda, with the so-called Gothic Orchestra on the left and the southern row of supper-boxes beyond. The view is populated by many identifiable visitors and performers, with parties at supper, gentlemen ogling young ladies, and a great deal of acute observation. Contemporary viewers would have instantly recognized a number of the individual figures. At the center of the composition are two of the most celebrated society beauties of the period, Georgiana, Duchess of Devonshire and her sister, Henrietta, Lady Duncannon.[5] By the early 1780s the sisters had become a favorite subject for Rowlandson's satire, as their extravagant and increasingly scandalous private lives filled the pages of the gossip newspapers. On the right, Rowlandson includes the actress Mary 'Perdita' Robinson and her husband, shown as a diminutive, elderly man with all the look of a cuckold.

A fact confirmed by the figure of George, Prince of Wales, Robinson's lover, whispering conspiratorially in her ear.

The audience are being entertained by the noted singer Mrs Weichsel, who is seen leaning from the orchestra, but most of the figures are engaged in a range of other activities. In the supper-box on the left viewers have traditionally identified Oliver Goldsmith, Samuel Johnson, Boswell and Mrs Thrale.[6] Although as Goldsmith died in 1774 it seems that this may be anecdotal rather than factual. Rowlandson certainly included prominent members of the press, including the proprietor and editor of the gossipy newspaper, *The World*, Captain Edward Topham who is seen an old fashioned macaroni, peering through his glass at the Duchess of Devonshire and the man dressed in a kilt to the right of the central group is almost certainly James Perry, editor

Thomas Rowlandson
*Vauxhall Gardens, c.*1784
Watercolour, pen and ink
19 × 29⅜ inches · 482 × 748 mm
© Victoria and Albert Museum

of *The London Gazette*. More figures are probably identifiable, but as with all of Rowlandson's greatest images it is less about personal satire, than a wry portrayal of London society and its foibles. Thus Rowlandson delights as much in depicting the orchestra, or the waiter struggling to uncork a bottle, as he does the bon ton.[7]

The success of Rowlandson's watercolour at the Academy made it an obvious candidate for publication by the burgeoning London print trade. The aquatint plate was made by Francis Jukes, who seems to have learnt the process from his friend Paul Sandby. Aquatint, a tonal method of etching, was perfect for rendering watercolours into print and had been pioneered in the 1770s by the French artist J.B. Le Prince and adapted for commercial

John Raphael Smith (1752–1812)
Portrait of Thomas Rowlandson
Black chalk, pencil and grey ink
10⅞ × 10¼ inches · 278 × 206 mm
© The Trustees of the British Museum

use in England by Sandby.[8] The plate was published by John Raphael Smith, one of the most successful and prolific print publishers of the 1780s, who exported impressions of Rowlandson's print across Europe. Smith continued to sell Rowlandson's print after the shock of the French Revolution suppressed the market and it is listed in a surviving catalogue he produced in 1798.[9]

As Henry Angelo noted in 1830, Vauxhall was still in print, its popularity making it one of Rowlandson's most successful compositions. The present sheet is extremely early, given the clarity and richness of the impression, probably made by Smith shortly after Jukes had completed the plate.

The present very early impression dating to soon after its publication in 1785, has been mounted on a sheet of Whatman paper for support, it is trimmed to outside the image and below the publication line but within the platemark. There is one vertical crease through the right side of the image and a few short tears and thinned area behind the address at bottom center. There is a small amount of surface dust in the margin at the bottom left but the image is otherwise pristine and displays a beautiful printed tone.

NOTES

1 See Matthew Payne and James Payne, *Regarding Thomas Rowlandson: 1757–1827; His Life, Art & Acquaintance*, London, 2010, pp.78–80.

2 For the most substantial account of Vauxhall see David Coke and Alan Borg, *Vauxhall Gardens, A History*, New Haven and London, 2011.

3 James Boswell, *Boswell's Life of Johnson*, London, 1851, pp.599–600.

4 *European Magazine*, V, April 1784, p.248. Another version of the watercolour is in the collection of the Yale Center for British Art. See John Baskett and Dudley Snelgrove, *The Drawings of Thomas Rowlandson in the Paul Mellon Collection*, no.12, pp.13–14.

5 See Matthew Payne and James Payne, *Regarding Thomas Rowlandson: 1757–1827; His Life, Art & Acquaintance*, London, 2010, p.78.

6 These identifications are upheld as 'indisputable' by Coke and Borg in their account of Rowlandson's composition see: David Coke and Alan Borg, *Vauxhall Gardens, A History*, New Haven and London, 2011, p.237–239.

7 This and Angelo's comment that Rowlandson, 'found plenty of employment for his pencil', is confirmed by the survival of a number of other drawings by Rowlandson of other subjects from Vauxhall Gardens, including a sheet showing acrobats at the gates (private collection).

8 See Richard T. Godfrey, *Printmaking in Britain: A General History from its Beginnings to the Present Day*, Oxford, 1978, p.58. For Sandby's pioneering use of aquatint see: Ann V. Gunn, Sandby, Greville and Burdett, and the 'Secret' of Aquatint,' *Print Quarterly*, XXIX, no.2, 2012, pp.178–180.

9 Ellen G. D'Oench, *Copper into Gold: Prints by John Raphael Smith, 1754–1812*, New Haven and London, 1999, Appendix III.

THOMAS STOTHARD RA 1755–1834

The Pilgrimage to Canterbury

Pen and ink over pencil with watercolour on Whatman Turkey Mill paper watermarked 1833
4 × 13½ inches · 99 × 344 mm

LITERATURE
Shelley M Bennett, *Thomas Stothard: the mechanisms of art patronage in England circa 1800*, 1988, p.47.

SUBJECT ENGRAVED
Louis Schiavonetti and James Heath, after Thomas Stothard, *The Pilgrimage to Canterbury*, 1809–17, etching and engraving
10½ × 37¾ inches · 268 × 933 mm
A fine impression on India paper with the engraved word 'Proof' accompanies the watercolour. First issue lettered proofs of this nature are of far superior quality to the normal lettered print impressions which lack the word 'Proof' and which have been re-printed from the plate up to the present day.

The present watercolour is Stothard's final version of his most famous picture, begun in the last of year of his life and left partially completed at his death in 1834. *The Pilgrimage to Canterbury* was one of the triumphs of early nineteenth-century history painting, exhibited all over Britain in 1807, admired by the public and critics alike and transformed into a best-selling engraving. Walter Scott endorsed it as 'executed with the genius and spirit of a master, and all the rigid attention to costume that could be expected of the most severe antiquary'. In addition to the original large oil (Tate Britain), Stothard was commissioned to make three copies in oil for admirers (including the poet Samuel Rogers)

and he also made several watercolour reductions, including the present example. While being three times smaller than the original, Stothard has successfully condensed, even intensified, the multiple details of the Pilgrims' expressions and costume in pen and ink, in a manner typical of his later works. Heightened with white, the final colouring of the Pilgrims and their horses has been left only partially completed, allowing an intense scrutiny of the elderly Stothard's disciplined line.

The original composition of *Canterbury Pilgrims was* commissioned by the engraver Robert Cromek in 1806. The painting was first exhibited at Cromek's house in London, then shown throughout England and Scotland, drawing large crowds at the admission price of one shilling per person and by May 1807 he could claim that three thousand people had seen and praised it. Cromek commissioned Louis Schiavonetti to engrave Thomas Stothard's composition, but when Schiavonetti died in 1810 he had completed only the etched state of the plate. The plate was finally completed by James Heath and was published on 1 October 1817 and was also enormously popular. It captured the contemporary appeal for Chaucer's work and the range of social and character types it celebrated. The highly energetic frieze-like composition acted as a compendium of Chaucer's characters. Its popularity involved Stothard in a bitter controversy with his friend, William Blake. In brief, Blake claimed that Cromek commissioned from him a painting illustrating Chaucer's story of the pilgrimage to Canterbury and after seeing his fresco sketch, Cromek withdrew the commission. According to Blake, Cromek then proceeded to commission from

Stothard a similar painting based on what he had seen in Blake's sketch.[1]

Most contemporary evidence, in particular accounts by John Thomas Smith in *Nollekens and His Times* and by Allan Cunningham in his *Lives of Eminent British Painters* support the view that Stothard was the true originator of both this concept and its design.[2] Both of these authors assert that Blake visited Stothard while the latter was working on his Chaucer design and stole the concept from Stothard. If true, it would seem that Blake then rushed to finish his engraving of the subject by 1810, ahead of plate after Stothard's painting – a view which would fit with Blake's continuing precarious financial predicament. Recent evidence suggests that Blake's plate was in fact a blatant plagiarism of Thomas Stothard's work.

Though Stothard continued to be productive into the 1830s, the watermark of 1833 dates the picture to very close to the accident in which he was hit by a carriage in the autumn of that year, leading to his disablement and ultimate death in 1834. In its clarity and freshness the present watercolour is a magnificent miniature version of Stothard's greatest work, a perfect distillation of a hugely popular subject and an early example of the power of mass-publicity and the print market, the two things which would power the London art market in the nineteenth century.

1 Shelley M. Bennett, *Thomas Stothard: The Mechanics of Patronage in England c.1800*, Columbia, 1988, p.46–49.
2 John Thomas Smith, *Nollekens and His Times*, London, 1828, II, pp.467–471 and Allan Cunningham, *Lives of Eminent British Painters*, London, 1829, II, p.163.

PILGRIMAGE TO CANTERBURY.

Dedicated by Permission to HIS ROYAL HIGHNESS THE *PRINCE REGENT*.
BY HIS ROYAL HIGHNESS'S
Most humbly devoted Subject and Servant,
GEELABETH CROMER.

Dédié par Permission spéciale À SON ALTESSE ROYALE LE *PRINCE REGENT*
Par la très humble et très Dévouée Servante et Sujette,
DE SON ALTESSE ROYALE
EGELABETH CROMER.

JOSEPH MALLORD WILLIAM TURNER 1775–1851

IAN WARRELL

The Farnley-Munro Sketchbook

The three sketchbook pages offered here belong to a larger group recently acquired by Lowell Libson that were formerly part of a sketchbook used by Turner in 1824, during his final visit to Farnley Hall, near Otley, This was the home of Walter Fawkes (1769–1825), who was the most significant patron of the first half of Turner's career. As well as acquiring several important oil paintings, such as *The Dort Packet-Boat from Rotterdam becalmed* (1818, Yale Center for British Art, New Haven), and the complete set of fifty views of the Rhine resulting from the 1817 tour, Fawkes commissioned many watercolours of his Yorkshire home and the surrounding estate. Turner had been a regular visitor there since 1808, but his stay at Farnley in 1824 (between 19 November and 14 December) proved to be his last because Fawkes died the following October, aged only 56. After that Turner could not be persuaded to visit the place again.

The book was then less than half full. But in preparing for a tour of the Alps in 1836, Turner packed it with the other materials he took with him. He was travelling that year with Hugh Andrew Johnstone Munro of Novar (1797–1864), a Scottish landowner, who was already establishing himself as the most notable collector of Turner's later works. The tour was intended to lift the spirits of the young Munro, and conferred on him the exceptional status of being one of only a handful of people permitted to travel with Turner. As an amateur artist, he also benefitted from the impromptu advice Turner offered when they were sketching in the Val d'Aosta. At some stage in the journey Munro found the Farnley sketchbook among his things. He recalled: 'I shewed it to Turner, who, after looking over it, again

put it into my hands. I suppose it had been originally put up to enable him to make use of the unused up paper in it'. Though this was clearly Turner's intention, none of the subjects in the sketchbook can be linked with the 1836 journey. But in giving the book to Munro, Turner was making a telling gesture, linking the two crucial friendships that had supported his work. Significantly, this was apparently the only time he ever gave away a sketchbook. Indeed, he generally went out of his way to prevent anyone seeing inside his working notebooks.

After leaving Munro's collection, when his estate was settled, the book belonged to the etcher John Postle Heseltine (1843–1929). A note he added in the front of the book indicates that he mistakenly thought the watercolours and sketches had been made as late as 1831, during Turner's extensive tour of Scotland. Turner had then stayed briefly at Munro's home, Novar House, in Evanton, which was perhaps one of the factors that induced Heseltine to link the book with this year.

After Heseltine's death, the book was sold at Sotheby's (29 May 1935, lot 366). It was subsequently exhibited in Birmingham, where the Art Gallery and Museum, were encouraged to buy it. However, it thereafter entered the collection of Allon Dawson of Leathley Grange, Ottley (1887–1965), with whose family it remained.

The Farnley-Munro sketchbook was made up of the standard Whatman paper that Turner habitually used and originally constituted 40 pages, though ultimately Turner painted or sketched on just half of these. Most of the images were painted on the 1824 trip to Yorkshire, but two sheets were used for views of Indian temples, perhaps in connection with a plan to illustrate Thomas Moore's *Lalla Rookh*, or they may have been inspired by the visit he made to the oriental splendour of the Royal Pavilion in Brighton that year.

Another notable feature of the book is its concentration on studies of the sky, and atmospheric effects, such as rainbows or stormy sunsets. These subtle and dramatic sketches of cloud formations should perhaps be related to the new interest in meteorology, and specifically the writings of Luke Howard (1772–1864), who had provided the first classification of cloud types. It is well known that in the early 1820s, cloud studies formed a distinct aspect of the work of John Constable. But Turner was similarly obsessed with the sky, if not in quite such a precise, quasi-scientific way as his rival. Indeed, the watercolours in this book develop, in a larger format, the observations made in the 'Skies' sketch-book (Turner Bequest CLVIII; Tate), which was in use in 1818.

Turner's biographer, Alexander J. Finberg, in an article for the *Connoisseur* in October 1935, was the first to link the images in the sketchbook with the last trip to Farnley. He comments there that the brooding sunset on the first sheet of the book lacks enough detail to link it with a specific location. However, the pencil sketch on the verso, in conjunction with those made in the vicinity of Farnley Hall on the following sheets, induced him to state 'we need have no hesitation in deciding that the sunset on the opening page represents the view looking over Lake Tiny at Farnley'. While this identification remains quite possible, the wide road in the foreground of the image could suggest that the effect was seen while Turner was en route up to Yorkshire. The building seen in silhouette on the right of the image might help to determine the precise location, but it is difficult to establish its scale: it could

[Fig.1] J.M.W. Turner
Sunset
Watercolour
12 × 18⅜ inches · 306 × 468 mm
© Tate, London 2013

[Fig.2] J.M.W. Turner
*Lindley Bridge and Hall,
on the Washburn*
Farnley folio 8, verso
Pencil
Private collection, formerly with
Lowell Libson Ltd

[Fig.3] J.M.W. Turner
*Caley Crags on the Chevin,
opposite Farnley*
Farnley folio 8, verso
Pencil
Private collection, formerly with
Lowell Libson Ltd

be a great church, or a barn. None of this detracts from the power of the image, which can be compared with some of the finest colour studies in the Turner Bequest (see TB CCLXIII 30; Tate D25428) [fig.1].

As Finberg noted, the pencil sketches on f.2 of the book are much easier to link with Farnley. When making the view on the front of the sheet, Turner held his book so that the outer, side edge was the top of the image, apparently planning to make a series of images moving down the page (as he did in other notebooks). Here Farnley Hall can be seen on the crown of the hill in the far distance, above the junction of the River Wharfe with its tributary, the Washburn, entering the main stream from the right [page 97].

Turning the page over, he made a view on the Washburn of a farm building with a distant bridge [page 96]. The sketch afterwards served as the basis for a watercolour, still in private hands, which has been called both *Lindley Bottom* and *Guy Barn, Bank and Ford, with Lindley Bridge* (see Andrew Wilton, *The Life and Work of J.M.W. Turner*, Fribourg 1979, p.372, no.624, dated '*c*.1818'). The tall trees, which form such an elegant repoussoir on the right of the finished watercolour, did not fit on the confines of f.2 verso, by the time Turner had set out most of his composition. Accordingly, he rolled his page back to add them to the back of f.1, completing his scene there [page 100].

Two further Farnley subjects can be found on f.8, sketched in opposite alignments [figs. 2–3]. One of these depicts the bridge over the Washburn leading up to Lindley Hall, another local property belonging to the Fawkes family. Once again, this is a subject that Turner developed as a finished watercolour (see Wilton 1979, p.372, no.623).

The other pencil sketch on f.8 shows a group of men up among the rocks of Caley Crags, on the other side of the Wharfe valley [fig.3]. One of the figures appears

to be steadying something that could be either a gun or a telescope. Fawkes and his guests often went shooting on the nearby moors known as the Chevin. This part of the sheet is marked by a blot of black wash, which may have been where Turner tested his brush while working on the image on the facing page, which showed a stage coach under a cloudy wintry sky, possibly at Wakefield (private collection; the watercolour is reproduced in Finberg's article).

A related study of contemporary modes of transport can be found on the other side of f.8, where Turner painted a wonderfully atmospheric image of a team of horses (or cattle) pulling a wagon down the hill from a windmill [fig.4]. Framing the whole scene is the arc of a huge rainbow, its form, but not its individual colours, represented as a beam of light on the unpainted paper (Another

sheet later in the book also depicted a rainbow among stormy clouds; f.13, private collection). The location of the mill in this haunting image is likely to be somewhere reasonably close to Farnley, but has not yet been pinpointed. In painting the scene, Turner uses a limited range of inky tones similar to those in many of the wash sketches his 'Old London Bridge' sketchbook at the Tate (Turner Bequest CCV; Tate). In both cases, the use of this restrained palette can be related to the work he was doing around this time on the experimental designs that were engraved in mezzotint, and which are misleadingly known as the 'Little Liber'. Turner had worked on a long series of 70 sepia-toned landscape mezzotints published as *Liber Studiorum* between 1807 until his departure for Italy in 1819. The later group – the 'Little Liber' – are primarily studies

[Fig.4] J.M.W. Turner
Landscape with a windmill (recto)
Watercolour (recto) and pencil (verso)
7¾ × 10½ inches · 197 × 267 mm
Private collection, formerly with Lowell Libson Ltd

of effects, like those in this book, and have been variously dated, but seem likely to have been under way by 1824. Indeed some pencil calculations by Turner that were written inside the front cover of this sketchbook seem to relate to the project.

The following page of the sketchbook (f.9) also utilized the dark washes for its rising foreground and for a tree, or shrub [page 95]. But beyond that the distant view is painted in pure prismatic colours: yellow for the area beside the river and for the bridge crossing it; blue for the shadows beyond the right hand foreground; and a glowing red for the moorland receding to the horizon. The scene is again near Farnley, with one of the bridges over the Wharfe.

Turner's Farnley studies continued at the other end of the sketchbook, suggesting that he flipped it round to begin again there. This enabled him to work on the sheet on the right hand side of each page opening, his preferred method in his sketchbooks. There were originally 5 studies of the River Washburn in this part of the book that were painted either wholly or primarily in brown, or sepia coloured washes. Most obviously, these recall the designs Turner had made for the *Liber Studiorum* plates. But during 1824 he would have seen the British Museum's newly acquired large group of drawings by Claude Lorrain, which were also painted in warm earthy tones. Many of those feature shady groves contrasted with sunlit glades, and seem to be an influence on the views Turner made on the Washburn while at Farnley. (see Ian Warrell, *Turner et le Lorrain*, exhibition catalogue, Musée des Beaux-Arts, Nancy, 2002, pp.126, 194).

One of these Washburn studies shows a curve in the river, with the bank of the opposite shore projecting across the foreground from the right side to create a snaking diagonal of light through the image [fig.5]. Restricting himself to his brown wash, Turner creates a rich range of tones and

[Fig.5] J.M.W. Turner
The River Washburn at Elsingbottom
Brown washes
7¾ × 10½ inches · 197 × 267 mm
Private Collection, formerly with
Lowell Libson Ltd

[Fig.6] J.M.W. Turner
Hunt in a wood
Pen and brown ink and brown wash
7⅝ × 10⅜ inches · 194 × 263 mm
© The Trustees of the
British Museum

[Fig.7] J.M.W. Turner
*Leathley Church, the River
Washburn in the foreground*
Pencil and sepia wash
7¾ × 10½ inches · 197 × 267 mm
Private collection, formerly with
Lowell Libson Ltd

half-tones, suggesting rocks in some places, bosky trees elsewhere, and drawing the eye upwards to the feathery foliage of the trees lining the river banks. He obviously enjoyed the shaded waters of this stream, probably spending time there pursuing his passion for angling. On an earlier visit to Farnley he had produced two larger watercolour studies of a similar character (see Wilton 1979, p.361, nos. 539, 540; both Yale Center for British Art, New Haven). Two related sepia studies from this book were exhibited by Agnew in 1987 (nos. 33, 41), while another sheet that seems to have been part of this group is now in the British Museum (1861,0810.31) [fig.6]. The latter is titled *Huntsmen in a Wood*, and has until now been lumped with the *Liber Studiorum*, when in fact it is summation of this group of studies, using its depiction of the trees bordering the Washburn to frame the church at Leathley. Like other sheets in the book, it has two pencil sketches on its verso, both of which seem to show the rocks of Caley Crags, like the scene on f.8.

The final sheet in this series is a view of Leathley Church, seen from the south, where the Washburn flows into the broader waters of the Wharfe [fig.7]. This beautifully subtle study is laid in over very faint pencil lines, indicating that Turner was setting out to record more diligently than elsewhere the specifics of the scene. His delicate use of the brush, and his fingertips, skillfully applied the paint to create a natural sense of depth, simultaneously leading the eye towards the brilliantly lit tower of the church (for a comparable work in the Turner Bequest, see TB CCIII N, Tate).

The empty binding of the Farnley Hall sketchbook and Munro's inscription on the inside cover.
Private collection, UK

JOSEPH MALLORD WILLIAM TURNER RA 1775–1851

Plein air study: the Wharfe Valley from the Chevin looking towards Otley Bridge & Farnley Hall

Watercolour
7¾ × 10½ inches, 197 × 267 mm
with a pencil sketch verso
From the Farnley-Munro sketchbook
(folio 9)

COLLECTIONS
H.A.J. Munro of Novar, a gift from Turner
in 1836, (d. 1865);
Isabella Munro-Johnstone, sister of the
above, d.1873;
Hon. Henry Butler, husband of the above,
d.1879;
Henry Alexander Munro-Butler-Johnstone,
son of the above, sold by 1880;
John Postle Heseltine, d.1929;
Mrs J.P. Heseltine, wife of the above, d.1935;
Lt. Col. Christopher Heseltine, sale, Sotheby,
3–5 June 1935, (an album of sketches by
Turner, £170);
Allon Dawson, acquired c.1935;
By family descent, 2013

LITERATURE
A. J. Finberg, 'Turner's newly identified
Yorkshire sketchbook', *The Connoisseur*,
October 1935, pp.185–7;
A. J. Finberg, *The Life of J.M.W. Turner*, 1961,
pp.286–7.

This richly evocative colour study demonstrates Turner's preoccupation with how best to communicate climate, light and landscape with watercolour wash. Technically inventive and highly informal, this sheet depicts a view close to Farnley Hall. David Hill has recently confirmed the viewpoint in this *plein air* study as being the steep West Chevin road, looking north-east over the bridge towards Farnley Hall itself. Hill also points out that Turner had made a drawing over ten years earlier of the same view from the same viewpoint in the 'Woodcock Shooting' sketchbook of *c.*1812–13 (Tate Britain, TB CXXIX 40a). It was probably made *en route* to Farnley or on an excursion from the house.

By 1824 Turner had spent a great deal visiting the Fawkes family at Farnley Hall and would have been intimately acquainted with the approaches to and from the house. It is clear from the surviving sketchbooks, finished watercolours and anecdotal details that Turner took an active part in the life of the household when staying. Turner seems to have been particularly keen on shooting, accompanying Fawkes and his party onto the neighbouring moors, as his earliest biographer Walter Thornbury noted:
It was on one of these occasions that, returning from shooting, nothing else would satisfy Turner but driving the present Mr Fawkes home a rough way, partly through fields, and in a tandem. Need I say that this precarious vehicle was soon capsized, amid shouts of good-humoured laughter? And henceforward, for that reason, Turner was known at Farnley by the nickname of 'Over-Turner'.[1]

As Ian Warrell has pointed out, in the essay in this catalogue, the Farnley Hall sketchbook demonstrates Turner's preoccupation with meteorology and light effects on landscape. This rich watercolour study is also technically innovative. Turner has saturated the page with water and then applied broad watercolour washes to the damp paper, imparting a diffuse, indistinct quality to the landscape. The highly atmospheric study is anchored by the solitary topographical element, Otley Bridge, in the middle-distance. Turner's familiarity with the moors around Farnley and his love of the landscape prompted him to make this impressive and highly impressionistic study.

Although now famous for these highly suggestive and modern looking studies, Turner would never have intended for sheets such as this to be exhibited. The majority of such works were contained in his sketchbooks – this page has not been trimmed and the stitching holes from the sketchbook binding are visible on the left-hand side – most of which remained in his studio at his death in 1851 when they were left to the nation. This sketchbook is the only example known to have been given away by Turner in his lifetime. He gave it to his friend and patron, Hugh Monro of Novar. In 1854, Gustav Waagen commented on the 'perfect treasury' of drawings by Turner in the Munro collection. It was acquired after Monro's death by John Postle Heseltine, one of the greatest collectors of English drawings in the late nineteenth century. The present sheet is therefore not only a highly sensitive and technically innovative celebration of Turner's friendship with Walter Fawkes, but in its provenance links two of the greatest collectors of Turner's work.

1 Walter Thornbury, *The Life of J.M.W. Turner RA*, London, 1862, II,p.85.

JOSEPH MALLORD WILLIAM TURNER RA 1775–1851

View on the Washburn looking towards Lindley Bridge

Pencil
7¾ × 10½ inches, 197 × 267 mm
Verso: *Farnley Hall from the River Wharfe*
From the Farnley-Munro sketchbook
(folio 2 and 2 verso)

COLLECTIONS
H.A.J. Munro of Novar, a gift from Turner
in 1836, (d. 1865);
Isabella Munro-Johnstone, sister of the
above, d.1873;
Hon. Henry Butler, husband of the above,
d.1879;
Henry Alexander Munro-Butler-Johnstone,
son of the above, sold by 1880;
John Postle Heseltine, d.1929;
Mrs J.P. Heseltine, wife of the above, d.1935;
Lt. Col. Christopher Heseltine, sale, Sotheby,
3–5 June 1935, (an album of sketches by
Turner, £170);
Allon Dawson, acquired in 1935;
By family descent, 2013

LITERATURE
A. J. Finberg, 'Turner's newly identified
Yorkshire sketchbook', *The Connoisseur*,
October 1935, pp.185–7;
A. J. Finberg, *The Life of J.M.W. Turner*, 1961,
pp.286–7

It was this fine sheet from the 1824 sketchbook which enabled A.J. Finberg to link it
definitively with Turner's trip to Farnley Hall
in Yorkshire. Farnley, situated west of York
near Otley, was the home of Walter Fawkes
the most important patron of the first half
of Turner's career. Fawkes acquired nearly
200 watercolours and six oils from the artist
in the period between 1808 and 1810, spending a total of £3,500 in the process.[1] But
Fawkes was more than a generous patron,
Turner seems to have been completely

accepted into his family life and his activities
in Yorkshire seem to have been as much social
as artistic. Walter Thornbury reported that
'there he shot and fished and was as playful as
a child.'[2]

Turner used folio 2 of the sketchbook
to record his first sight of Farnley Hall.
Turning the page so it was portrait, rather
than landscape, and working from the outer
edge of the page, Turner was apparently
planning to make a series of images moving
down the page, a method for making rapid
sketches which he had used before. The
drawing depicts Farnley Hall on the crown of
the hill in the far distance, above the junction
of the River Wharfe with its tributary, the
Washburn, entering the main stream from
the right. On the verso of the sheet, Turner
made a view on the Washburn of a farm
building with a distant bridge. Turner was
evidently planning an expansive, panoramic
landscape, as the trees on the left-hand side
spilled on to the verso of f.1. The sketch afterwards served as the basis for a watercolour,
still in private hands, which has been called
both *Lindley Bottom* and *Guy Barn, Bank and
Ford, with Lindley Bridge*.[3]

These confident and incisive pencil studies
demonstrate Turner's ability to capture the
familiar Yorkshire landscape with a remarkable economy of line. In contrast to the two
watercolour studies from the sketchbook,
Turner here shows his sensitivity to form
and tone without the use of colour. Walter
Fawkes, at Farnley Hall between 19th
November and 14th December 1824. Turner
was unable to bear returning to Farnley after
Fawkes's death in 1825, making the recto
study of the hall Turner's last record of the
house he had spent so much time in the first
decades of his career.

verso: *Farnley Hall from the River Wharfe*

J.M.W. Turner *Farnley Hall*
Pencil · 4¼ × 7 inches · 110 × 178 mm
From the Devon Rivers, No.2 sketchbook, *c*.1812–5
© Tate, London 2013 (T.B. CXXXIII 77)

NOTES

1　See David Hill, *Turner in Yorkshire*, exh.cat.
York (York City Art Gallery), 1980, p.7.
2　Walter Thornbury, *The Life of J.M.W.
Turner RA*, London, 1862, II, p.85.
3　Andrew Wilton, *The Life and Work of J.M.W.
Turner*, Fribourg, 1979, p.372, no.624.

JOSEPH MALLORD WILLIAM TURNER RA 1775–1851

A plein air study at sunset: Farnley, Yorkshire

Watercolour
7¾ × 10½ inches, 197 × 267 mm
with a pencil sketch verso
From the Farnley-Munro sketchbook of 1824
(folio 1, with a pencil sketch verso, continuing the sketch on f.2 verso)

COLLECTIONS
H.A.J. Munro of Novar, a gift from Turner in 1836, (d. 1865);
Isabella Munro-Johnstone, sister of the above, d.1873;
Hon. Henry Butler, husband of the above, d.1879;
Henry Alexander Munro-Butler-Johnstone, son of the above, sold by 1880;
John Postle Heseltine, d.1929;
Mrs J.P. Heseltine, wife of the above, d.1935;
Lt. Col. Christopher Heseltine, sale, Sotheby, 3–5 June 1935, (an album of sketches by Turner, £170);
Allon Dawson, acquired in 1935;
By family descent, 2013

LITERATURE
A. J. Finberg, 'Turner's newly identified Yorkshire sketchbook', *The Connoisseur*, October 1935, pp.185–7;
A. J. Finberg, *The Life of J.M.W. Turner*, 1961, pp.286–7

This highly atmospheric watercolour depicts a sunset at Farnley and was the first page in the sketchbook, and is one of the most highly finished and evocative sheets. A.J. Finberg identified the location, on the basis of the pencil study of Farnley Hall on f.2, as a 'view looking over Lake Tiny at Farnley.' As Ian Warrel discusses in his essay in this catalogue, this identification remains quite possible, the wide road in the foreground of the image could suggest that the effect may have been seen while Turner was *en route* up to Yorkshire. The building seen in silhouette on the right of the image might help to determine the precise location, but it is difficult to establish its scale. None of this detracts from the power of the image, which can be compared with some of the finest colour studies in the Turner Bequest.

Turner visited Farnley Hall on a number of occasions between 1808 and Walter Fawkes's death in 1825. As a result Turner became extremely familiar with the surrounding landscape. As Turner's early biographer Walter Thornbury noted: *Farnley Hall looks down on the Wharfe, the river that flows beneath the walls of Bolton Abbey, one of Turner's favourite scenes. Those roundel scaurs that he all his life delighted in, and to some semblance of which he ever moulded the eternal Alps, stretch in a misty and sun-barred line opposite the peacock-guarded terraces of the fine old Carolan hall.*[1]

Whilst the present watercolour probably shows the moorland near Farnley Hall, rather than the 'scaurs' or steep slopes on the river Wharfe, Turner's familiarity with the landscape afforded him the freedom to produce this highly concentrated study of a brooding sunset without concerning himself too much with details of topography. Turner

has captured the prismatic quality of the setting sun with feathery brush-strokes of watercolour contrasting it with the inky silhouette of trees on the horizon, which all contributes to impart a remarkable sense of atmosphere to the study. The immediacy of this *plein air* work is emphasised by the abraded area on the left, caused by wetting the paper and then scratching out, it is not clear if this was done by accident or design. This watercolour study belongs to Turner's most experimental and intense body of colour sketches. It shows both his technical mastery of watercolour as a medium and the intensity of his response to the familiar Yorkshire landscape.

As Ian Warrell outlined in his introductory essay these studies were originally part of a now dismembered sketchbook that Turner gave to his close friend Hugh Munro of Novar. A piece of paper pasted inside the front cover of the sketchbook recorded in Munro's hand:

When I traveled in 1836 with Turner through France, Switzerland and the Val d'Aosta I found this sketchbook amongst my things – I showed it to Turner, who after looking over it, again put it into my hands – I suppose it had been originally put up to enable him to make use of the unused paper in it.

It was Finberg's supposition that Turner's housekeeper had included the partially used sketchbook in Turner's luggage in 1836 as she noticed that it was only half-filled and that when he looked at it again on tour, overcome by poignant memories, he made the uncharacteristic gesture of giving it to Munro, Fawkes's successor as Turner's confidant. The sketchbook then passed to John Postle Heseltine, one of the greatest collectors of English drawing at the end of the nineteenth century. This sheet therefore not only represents the mature Turner exploring atmospheric effects in watercolour, but links three of the greatest connoisseurs of Turner's work.

1   Walter Thornbury, *The Life of J.M.W. Turner* RA, London, 1862, ii,p.85.

verso

BENJAMIN WEST PRA 1738–1820

Mrs Shute Barrington

Black and white chalk on grey prepared paper, squared
8⅝ × 6¾ inches · 220 × 171 mm
Signed lower left: *B West*
Drawn in 1808

LITERATURE
Helmut von Erffa and Allen Staley, *The Paintings of Benjamin West*, New Haven and London, 1986, cat.no.589, p.488.

Despite his large graphic output comparatively few drawings by West relating to specific portraits survive. The present sheet, a sensitive study for the painting of *Mrs Shute Barrington* of 1808, is therefore an important addition to West's *oeuvre*, being published here for the first time.

By 1800 West, who had been elected the second President of the Royal Academy of Arts on the death of Sir Joshua Reynolds in 1792, was one of the most prominent painters in Britain. Although his practice was largely historical – he had been made historical painter to King George III in 1772 and was responsible for decorating the interiors of Windsor Castle with paintings of scenes from British history – West was also a successful and productive portrait

Benjamin West
The Honorable Mrs. Shute Barrington, 1808
Oil on canvas · 50 × 40 inches · 1270 × 1015 mm
Signed and dated lower left: *B. West 1808*
Cummer Gallery of Art, Jacksonville, Florida
Foundation Purchase, AP.1960.2.1.

painter. The present study is for the portrait of *Jane Barrington*, now in the Cummer Gallery of Art, Jacksonville, Florida, which is signed and dated 1808. The sitter was born Jane Guise in 1733, the the daughter of Sir John Guise, Bt., she married the Hon. Shute Barrington, then Bishop of Llandaff in 1770. Barrington was subsequently made Bishop of Salisbury and finally Durham in 1791, where Jane Barrington died in 1807.

In the finished portrait *Mrs Shute Barrington* is depicted seated, her left hand resting on a bible, with a distant view of the west front of Durham Cathedral visible through the window. There has been some confusion over the precise date of the finished portrait; William Roberts suggested that it was executed at the time of the Barrington's marriage, the view of Durham and West's signature being added in 1808, whilst von Erffa and Staley noted that the handling of the portrait was consistent with West's work in 1808.[1] This supposition is supported by the present drawing which includes Durham Cathedral, confirming the whole composition was conceived at the same moment, a fact further supported by our discovery of a receipt for the painting dated January 1809 and preserved in Durham Cathedral Library, which is printed here for the first time.

The unusual circumstances of the commission probably prompted the completion of this sensitively handled drawing. The study is rendered in black chalk on grey prepared paper, heightened with white chalk and has an immediacy and engaging quality lost in the finished painting. West completed similar studies for other portraits where the sitters were no longer living, for example his 1797 portrait of *Peter Beckford*,

Charles Turner, after Sir Thomas Lawrence
The Honble and Right Reverend Shute Barrington,
1817
Mezzotint · 21⅞ × 16 inches · 557 × 406 mm
© The Trustees of the British Museum

the seventeenth-century ancestor of William Beckford.[2] The newly discovered letter from Barrington to West suggests that *Mrs Shute Barrington* was being painted as a pendant to an existing portrait of the Bishop which was being reframed to make them a pair. Von Erffa and Staley, without knowing this document, suggested the portrait was paired with one by Sir Thomas Lawrence now at Merton College, Oxford on the basis of their identical dimensions.[3] This drawing therefore throws important light on West's working method, as well as being a highly significant addition to his known work.

Durham Cathedral Library and Archive[4]
Add Ms 255/6a-b
Shute Barrington to Benjamin West,
20 January, 1809:
Cav: Square 20 Jan. 1809
The Bishop of Durham presents comps to Mr West, & sends here: with a draft on Messrs. Drummond for an hundred guineas: which he will be so good as to acknowledge.

The Bishop requests the favour of Mr West to permit the two pictures to remain where they are till the end of April; by wh. time the Bishop desires that the new frame for Bishop Barrington's portrait may be ready.

NOTES

1 William Roberts, 'The Honourable Mrs Shute Barrington by Benjamin West, PRA, 1738–1820 Painted for Bishop Shute Barrington, and hung at their estate, Mongewell Park, Oxon', unpublished typescript, 1920, Frick Art Reference Library; Helmut von Erffa and Allen Staley, *The Paintings of Benjamin West*, New Haven and London, 1986, cat.no.589, p.488.

2 West's portrait of *Peter Beckford* was sold Sotheby's November 24, 2005, lot. 70. The preparatory drawing is preserved at Swarthmore College, Pennsylvania.

3 Barrington seems to have compulsively sat for portraits as examples exist by: Sir Thomas Lawrence (Merton College, Oxford and Auckland Castle, Bishop Auckland); William Owen (Newcastle Hospitals, Newcastle and Balliol College, Oxford); Richard Evans (Durham University, Durham); John Opie (University of Oxford, Oxford) and George Romney (private collection).

4 We are extremely grateful to Gabriel Sewell, Head of Collections at Durham Cathedral, for providing a transcription of this document.

JOSEPH WRIGHT OF DERBY 1734–1797

Mount Vesuvius

Pencil and black chalk
12½ × 16½ inches · 308 × 420 mm
Signed and dated: *J. Wright delin 1775* (lower
left), also inscribed lower centre:
*Mount Vesuvius/Drawing was made by Wright
of Derby when in Italy in 1775*

COLLECTIONS
Probably in Wright's studio at his death,
inscribed by his executor John Holland
of Ford, who probably passed it to one of
Wright's friends;
Sir Gilbert Inglefield, by 1968;
Private collection, 2006.

LITERATURE
B. Nicolson, *Joseph Wright of Derby: Painter
of Light*, London, 1968, 1, p.76 and 2, p.101,
pl.165.

Richard Hurleston (fl. 1763–1780)
Joseph Wright of Derby, 1774–6
Oil on canvas
26½ × 22¼ inches · 673 × 565 mm
Yale Center for British Art, Paul Mellon Collection

'Tis the grandest effect
I ever painted [1]

This hugely significant drawing has been
surprisingly overlooked by scholars
of Wright's Grand Tour since its first
publication by Nicolson in 1968.[2] Probably
made on the spot in 1774–5 it shows the
spectacular eruption of the volcano
Mount Vesuvius at night and formed the
compositional study for one of Wright's
most celebrated paintings of the subject,
now in the Tate Gallery, London. This sheet
seems to have remained in Wright's studio
until his death and is one of a very small
number of highly finished drawings which
he continued to use long after his return
from the Continent. As such, it is not only a
highly sophisticated and unusually finished
drawing by Wright of one of the great
subjects of sublime landscape painting, but
key, previously overlooked, evidence of his
working method.

Wright travelled to Italy with his pregnant
wife, his student Richard Hurleston, and the
painter John Downman in November 1773.
He was already established in Britain as a
successful painter of 'candle-light' subjects,
thus rather than the purely educational tour
undertaken by young painters, the thirty-
nine year old Wright saw his European
trip as a commercial opportunity. Arriving
in Rome with paintings he had executed
back in Britain, Wright determined to
find patrons in Italy to support his Grand
Tour, noting in a letter to his brother: '[m]y
pictures are in great estimation here I am
shortly to be introduced to the Pope; & it is
thought he will honour me with a medal.'[3]
He must also have seen it as an opportunity
to acquire the classical vocabulary – derived

from both celebrated old masters and
antique sculpture – which would enable him
to triumph as a history painter at the newly
founded exhibiting societies in London.

Wright experimented with producing
historical scenes which utilized this classical
vocabulary, but it was the Italian landscape
which prompted his most successful and
enduring work. Like many visitors to
Rome he was struck by the profusion, scale
and quality of antique remains, but as his
surviving correspondence testifies, it was
the countryside and light that struck him
most, writing to his sister Nancy in May 1774,
he noted: '[t]he natural scenes are beautiful
and uncommon with an Atmosphere so
pure & Clear that objects 20 miles distant
seem not half the way.'[4] In October Wright
travelled to Naples, as he wrote to his
brother, Richard: 'to satisfy my curiosity
for seeing one of the most wonderful parts
of the world.'[5] Whilst there he visited
Mount Vesuvius, informing his brother on
his return to Rome that: 'there was a very
considerable Eruption at the time, of w.^ch
I am going to make a picture – Tis the most
wonderful sight in nature.'[6] Wright had
completed the painting by May the following year, when he wrote to his sister that 'tis
the grandest effect I ever painted', hoping
that it would be acquired through 'Mr
Baxter the Russian Consul' for Catherine the
Great at 100 guineas.[7] The sale fell-through
and this early Vesuvius painting can no
longer be identified with certainty.[8] At the
same date Wright was apparently working
on a view of the 'summit of the mountain'
which one contemporary noted: 'shows
more abilities in the terrible way, but does
not hurt Volaire', a work which is also now
lost.[9] These references to paintings made

Joseph Wright of Derby
Vesuvius in Eruption, c.1776–80
Oil on canvas · 48 × 69½ inches · 1220 × 1764 mm
© Tate, London 2013

back in Rome make it clear that Wright must have executed a number of drawn studies of Vesuvius whilst in Naples, of which the present sheet must be one.

Wright's interest in Vesuvius was a natural one. The fragment of a travel diary which survives in Derby Local Studies Library reveals that he was studious in viewing the royal collections in Naples, visiting the ancient towns destroyed by the volcano, Herculaneum and Pompeii, and the great museum founded to house the discoveries from their excavation at Portici.[10] It seems almost certain that he met Sir William Hamilton at this date. Hamilton was the British Minister Plenipotentiary to the court at Naples and one of the most noted connoisseurs and natural historians resident in Italy. In the 1770s he was in the midst of preparing his great illustrated

publication on Vesuvius, *The Campi Phlegraei,* which appeared in 1776. Hamilton's own copy, preserved in the British Library, contains an inscription claiming that Wright was actually involved in producing the illustrations.[11] Whilst this cannot be substantiated, it suggests that Hamilton may well have facilitated Wright's access to the volcano and acted as his guide. This may in turn explain a comment in one of Wright's letters to his brother, where he asks: 'when you see Whitehurst tell him I wished for his Company when on Mount Vesuvius, his thoughts wou'd have enter'd the bowels of the mountain mine skimed over the surface only.'[12] John Whitehurst was a fellow of the Royal Society, geologist and instrument maker who was passionately interested in volcanoes and whose theories and knowledge would perhaps have made

Mount Vesuvius

This Drawing was made by Wright of Derby when in Italy in 1775

Mount Vesuvius

This Drawing was made by Wright of Derby when in Italy in 1775

him a more appropriate companion for Hamilton than Wright.[13]

Hamilton's publication was prompted, at least in part, by the enormous interest in Vesuvius amongst scientists and *virtuosi* across Europe. No less fascinated were the countless Grand Tourists who visited Naples stimulating a flourishing trade in images and accounts of the volcano, its activities and victims. It was a market Wright was keen to exploit. Seven drawn studies by Wright of Vesuvius survive in total, all but the present sheet, held in the Derby Museum and Art Gallery. All but one of these studies, which will be discussed below, show the volcano during the day. They are either strictly topographical, such as the *Terrain near Vesuvius*, a black chalk drawing which concentrates on the rock formations (the caldera) adjacent to the summit, or show Vesuvius in the wider landscape of the plain. The present drawing is therefore unique in showing the volcano erupting and significantly, depicting this activity at night. Wright shows Vesuvius from its foothills looking south, the Bay of Naples on the right of the composition, the promontory to the left is Sorrento, and the island to the right of it is Capri. The drawing is the only one of Wright's surviving studies to capture the theatricality and drama inherent in the scene, a quality which was essential to its contemporary appeal.[14] Once back in Britain Wright paired paintings of Vesuvius with one of a firework display at Castel Sant' Angelo in Rome – known as La Girondola – commenting in a letter from Bath in 1776: 'As to the picture of Vesuvius the Town rings with commendation of it … I have just now finished a companion to it. The Exhibition of a great fire work from the castle of St. Angelo in Rome, the one is the greatest effect of Nature the other of Art that I suppose can be.'[15]

Wright eventually completed some thirty paintings of Vesuvius erupting, by far his most popular and commercially successful subject. It therefore seems remarkable that the present drawing, his most complete and dramatic study of the volcano, has received so little critical attention, especially as the

Joseph Wright of Derby
Study of Terrain near Vesuvius, 1774-5
Black chalk over pencil · 13⅝ × 19 inches; 346 × 483 mm
Derby Museum and Art Gallery

Joseph Wright of Derby
Vesuvius, 1774
Black chalk over pencil · 14⅝ × 20⅛ inches · 372 × 511 mm
Derby Museum and Art Gallery

survival of this sheet raises several important questions about Wright's technique. Nothing has been written about Wright's reliance on 'models' for producing later repetitions of popular compositions. If we accept that Wright completed no 'on the spot' painting of the eruption of Vesuvius then the present drawing must be seen as the most substantial and significant surviving study Wright made of the subject and one which stayed by him for the next twenty years as he completed new iterations of the subject.[16]

Whilst three sketchbooks and a number of powerful independent studies from nature survive from Wright's Grand Tour, the present drawing is unusual in being a highly worked-up compositional study for a painting. Only three other drawings of comparable finish and complexity survive from Wright's Italian stay. They comprise a pair of sheets depicting a grotto in the Gulf of Salerno in the morning and evening (private collection) and another nocturnal view of Vesuvius (Derby Museum and Art Gallery). The two views of grottos correspond directly to two pictures completed in Italy in 1774.[17] More instructively, the two drawings were used by Wright back in Britain as the model for historical works. Adding, for example, a group of banditti to the grotto at sunset in a painting dated 1778 (Museum of Fine Arts, Boston) recasting the pure landscape as a narrative work. The present drawing of Vesuvius fulfilled the same function. The painting which is closest to the study, now in the Tate Gallery, London, was executed in about 1780. Wright followed the preparatory drawing closely but added a steep bank in the foreground and two classical figures carrying a body,

thus transforming the scene into a depiction of the death of Pliny.

Given their utility it is perhaps not surprising to find each of these finished sheets recorded in Wright's collection at the time of his death when they were given by his executor, John Holland, to Wright's closest friends and professional associates. The two views of the grotto were given by Holland to Wright's patron, John Leigh Philips, a Manchester cotton manufacturer who owned a large number of Wright's most complex landscapes.[18] Their gift is recorded in a remarkable letter from Holland to Philips dated 16 January 1798. In it, Holland complained that:

We folks in trust are by no means competent to value drawings, & tho I may almost call myself an enthusiast in the oils, yet as I have not seen London or an auction of drawings for this last thirty years, how should I be adequate to the business.[19]

Wright's pupil and copier, the Manchester based painter William Tate was apparently: 'desirous to have some of Mr Wrights drawings … more particularly of his landscape = sketches.' We know Holland resolved against a sale of Wrights drawings, as an auction of his pictures took place in London in 1801 and Derby in 1810.[20] Holland seems instead to have dispersed Wright's drawings to his friends and professional associates. Along with the two Leigh Philips sheets, the Derby view of Vesuvius was given, along with another drawing of Vesuvius, to the Revd. Thomas Gisborne, Wright's close friend and sketching partner who lived near to Derby on the edge of the Needwood Forest. In establishing the possible provenance of the present drawing the Gisborne sheets offer significant evidence.

Both are inscribed by Gisborne himself. The first: 'This drawing was done by Mr Wright of Derby and was given to Mr Gisborne by Mr Holland of Ford' and the second: 'Chalk drawing of Mount Vesuvius by Mr Wright. The drawing was passed through a rolling press to fix the chalk.'[21]

The present sheet is inscribed in a different hand, which thanks to his surviving correspondence, can be identified as that of John Holland himself. Holland is likely therefore to have retained the drawing as a personal memento of his friendship with Wright. Holland had been an active and highly competent copyist of his friend's late landscapes and so, despite his claim not to be a competent judge of drawings, he must have understood their importance and value artistically.[22] This complex, highly sophisticated and extraordinarily beautiful drawing offers important evidence of Wright's working method in Italy and the method he used to complete the numerous repetitions of his most popular Continental subjects. More than this, the sheet is one of the most immediate and impressive graphic depictions of the eruption of Vesuvius, made by one of the finest painters of the eighteenth century.

NOTES

1 Joseph Wright to Nancy Wright, Rome, 4 May, 1775. See: Elizabeth Barker, 'Documents Relating to Joseph Wright 'of Derby' (1734–97)', *The Walpole Society*, LXI, 2009, p.85.

2 Wright's time in Rome has received comparatively little attention from scholars, the present drawing has only been published by Benedict Nicholson. See under literature.

3 Joseph Wright to Richard Wright, Rome, 10 August, 1774. See: Elizabeth Barker, 'Documents Relating to Joseph Wright 'of Derby' (1734–97)', *The Walpole Society*, LXI, 2009, p.82.

4 Joseph Wright to Nancy Wright, Rome, 22 May, 1774. See: Elizabeth Barker, 'Documents Relating to Joseph Wright 'of Derby' (1734–97)', *The Walpole Society*, LXI, 2009, p.80.

5 Joseph Wright to Richard Wright, Rome, 11 November, 1774. See: Elizabeth Barker, 'Documents Relating to Joseph Wright 'of Derby' (1734–97)', *The Walpole Society*, LXI, 2009, p.84.

6 Joseph Wright to Richard Wright, Rome, 11 November, 1774. See: Elizabeth Barker, 'Documents Relating to Joseph Wright 'of Derby' (1734–97)', *The Walpole Society*, LXI, 2009, p.84.

7 Joseph Wright to Nancy Wright, Rome, 2 May, 1775. See: Elizabeth Barker, 'Documents Relating to Joseph Wright 'of Derby' (1734–97)', *The Walpole Society*, LXI, 2009, p.85.

8 For the most comprehensive discussion of Wright's Vesuvius pictures see Benedict Nicolson, *Joseph Wright of Derby: Master of Light*, New Haven and London, 1968, I, Appendix B, pp.279–284.

9 Benedict Nicolson, *Joseph Wright of Derby: Master of Light*, New Haven and London, 1968, I, p.79.

10 Elizabeth Barker, 'Documents Relating to Joseph Wright 'of Derby' (1734–97)', *The Walpole Society*, LXI, 2009, pp.64–65.

11 London, British Library, Tab.435.a.15.

12 Joseph Wright to Richard Wright, Rome, 11 November, 1774. See: Elizabeth Barker, 'Documents Relating to Joseph Wright 'of Derby' (1734–97)', *The Walpole Society*, LXI, 2009, p.84.

13 For Whitehurst and his relationship with Wright and his landscapes, see: David Fraser, 'Fields of Radiance: the scientific and industrial scenes of Joseph Wright', in ed. Denis Cosgrove and Stephen Daniels, *The Iconography of Landscape,* Cambridge, 1988, pp.124–134.

14 This was a fact recognised by Nicolson, who noted that Vesuvius is seen: 'by moonlight with a view over the still sea, where he is not so much concerned with the texture of rock, as with its wavy sweep across the foreground.' Nicolson, *Joseph Wright of Derby: Master of Light*, New Haven and London, 1968, I, p.76.

15 Joseph Wright to Richard Wright, Bath, 15 January, 1776. See: Elizabeth Barker, 'Documents Relating to Joseph Wright 'of Derby' (1734–97)', *The Walpole Society*, LXI, 2009, p.88.

16 The present author has difficulty accepting the small gouache study of the erupting Vesuvius in the Derby Museum and Art Gallery which has no provenance beyond the early twentieth century. It was accepted by Nicolson and Egerton, but has never been the subject of serious consideration.

17 See Judy Egerton, *Joseph Wright of Derby*, exh. cat. London, (Tate Gallery), 1990, cat.nos.97 & 98, pp.159–161.

18 Amongst the large number of pictures Wright sold to Philips recorded in his Account Book, are: 'A sketch of Mount Vesuvius Evening to L. Philips', £10.10. But 'sketch' in this context is almost certainly a small oil work as opposed to a drawing. See Benedict Nicolson, *Joseph Wright of Derby: Painter of Light*, New Haven and London, I, Appendix B, no's 24–27, p.283.

19 Derby, Local Studies Library, MS 9862: John Holland to John Leigh Philips, 'Ford, near Chesterfield, Derbyshire', January 16, 1798.

20 William Bemrose, *The Life and Works of Joseph Wright, ARA, commonly called 'Wright of Derby'*, London, 1885, p.107 and 112.

21 Jane Wallis, *Joseph Wright of Derby, 1734 – 1797*, exh.cat., Derby (Derby Museum and Art Gallery), 1997, cat. no's. 122 and 123, p.80.

22 Numerous references to Holland copying Wright's works survive, including a number of the copies themself. See: Deborah. M. Brown, *A question of attribution: Eight British landscape paintings given to Joseph Wright of Derby (1734–1797) in the Queen's University Art Collection*, Unpublished Master's thesis, Queen's University, Kingston, Ontario, 1990, pp.53–85.

JOHAN ZOFFANY 1733–1810

Elephants Fighting

Black, white and red chalk
on blue-grey paper
9 × 16½ inches · 230 × 420 mm
Drawn *circa* 1784–8

COLLECTIONS
Johan Zoffany;
Zoffany sale, George Robins, 9th May 1811,
*A Catalogue of A Most Curious and Unique
Assemblage of the Valuable Property of the
distinguished artist, Johan Zoffany, Esq. Decd.,
Member of the Royal Academy …* , presumably
part of lot. 32 [Drawings in Chalk, illustra-
tive of the country and manner of India – by
Mr Zoffany] three, Elephants Fighting and
2 Views.';
Private collection, UK, 2013

LITERATURE
Mary Webster, *Johan Zoffany*, New Haven
and London, 2011, p.490.

This rare drawing depicts an elephant fight
at Lucknow and was made by Johan Zoffany
during his residence in the city in the 1780s.
Only a small number of Zoffany's Indian
drawings survive making the discovery of
this previously unrecorded example a highly
important addition to Zoffany's oeuvre.
More than this, it is a beautifully sensitive
rendering of a Moghul court entertainment,
made by a European artist

Johan Zoffany departed for India in 1783,
as Paul Sandby noted, where he 'anticipates
to roll in gold dust.'[1] He was given permission to travel by the East India Company
in the capacity of a portrait painter and
he must have hoped that his success at the
Courts of Europe in the previous decades
would be replicated in British controlled
Calcutta. Indeed the roll-call of patrons he
did attract suggests that his financial predic-
tions were correct, shortly after arriving,
he produced portraits of: Warren Hastings,
Elijah Impey, Claude Martin, Asaf-ud-Daula.
Although he established a successful practice
amongst Europeans in Calcutta, his most
engaging and important work emanated
from the time he spent 'up-country'.

Zoffany left Calcutta for Lucknow in 1784
where he remained until 1786. Lucknow was
the capital of Awadh, outside the territory
administered directly by the East Indian
Company, although within its sphere of
influence. Ruled by the Nawab Vizier of the
Mughal Empire, Asaf-ud-daula, it was the
home to a cultured and splendid court which
included a number of prominent Europeans,
most significantly Colonel Claude Martin
and Lieutenant-Colonel John Mordaunt.
Zoffany painted official portraits of Asaf-
ud-daula and his chief minister Hasan Reza
Khan and undertook his most famous Indian

composition in the city: *Colonel Mordaunt's Cock Match*. This monumental, multi-figure composition depicted a cockfight held between birds owned by Asaf-ud-daula and his favourite, Mordaunt. It depicts the court at play, incorporating portraits of the principal courtiers and members of the European diaspora in Awadh, including a self-portrait of Zoffany himself, the painter Ozias Humphry and Claude Martin.

Zoffany returned to Lucknow on the eve of his departure from India in 1787, he stayed with Martin at the house he had built close to the city, known now as Farhad Baksh. As Mary Webster has noted: 'from this moment he began to penetrate more deeply into Indian life, and to be captivated by its strangeness.'[2] It was on this later trip that Zoffany began to develop an interest in the Indian landscape, producing a number of distinctive drawings in

black, red and white chalks on a blue paper (which has turned a distinctive green-grey). The surviving drawings are principally topographical, documenting his return journey from Lucknow to Calcutta down the Ganges. These sheets show the buildings and incidents he witnessed along the river, from the dilapidated structures on Martin's estate at *Najafgarh* (Ashmolean Museum, Oxford), to the death of a Hindu at the ghats of Ghazipur (Yale Center for British Art, New Haven). They are considered some of the most evocative and sensitive landscape drawings made by a European artist in India during the eighteenth century.

It has long been known that the hand-full of examples which survive represent only a portion of the drawings Zoffany made in India. The posthumous auction of his studio, conducted by 'Messrs Robins' in May 1811 contained a considerable number

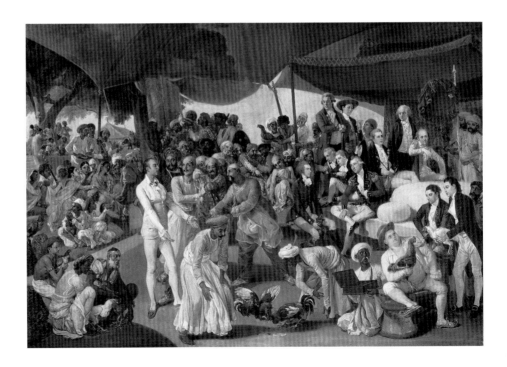

Johan Zoffany
*Colonel Mordaunt's Cock Match, c.*1784–6
Oil on canvas · 40⅞ × 59 inches · 1039 × 1500 mm
© Tate, London 2013

of studies listed as: 'drawings in chalks, illustrative of the country and manners of India – by Mr Zoffany.' The lot descriptions include 'twenty-one Elephants and Horses' and 'Seven, Natives of India', one lot in particular is listed as: 'Thee, Elephants Fighting, and 2 Views'.[3] This is almost certainly the lot which included the present drawing which depicts a fight between two elephants, rendered in Zoffany's customary mixed chalks on blue paper. The sheet depicts a magnificent spectacle at the court of Asaf-ud-daula, the ruler of Awadh and was almost certainly made at Lucknow. We know that such entertainments were a frequent part of the life of the court. As Lord Cornwallis, the Governor General of India noted disapprovingly of Asaf-ud-daula: 'I hear the wuzir extorts every rupee he can from his ministers to squander in debaucheries, cock-fighting, elephants and horses.'[4] But this dismissive view was not shared by many of the Europeans who were witness to the magnificence, as Mary Webster has noted: 'specialities of the court were combats held between large animals … India drew out in Zoffany a sporting side and elephants appear to have fascinated him.'[5]

Whilst there is no previous record of Zoffany attending an elephant fight, the following year the landscape painter William Daniell, travelling with his uncle Thomas, recorded in his diary on 18 July that: *Col. Martin, Un[cle]. & self went very early to the Nawaub's Bungalow at Gow Gautee to see the Elephant fight. The Nawaub gave us breakfast in the English stile. There were abt. 6 or 7 Engagements some of them very fierce. Un the rest of the day making a Sketch of the fight on a half length.*[6]

Gow Gautee was the complex Asaf-ud-daula built north of his main palace and on the south bank of the river Gompti which flows through Lucknow. The Daniells made a study of the fight which they later turned into a print to illustrate the second volume of their *Oriental Annual* in 1835. The text composed by the Reverend Hobart Caunter contained a description of the elephant fight which precisely corresponds to the action depicted by Zoffany in his drawing. Caunter's text relates how the Daniells: 'repaired to the veranda to see a specimen of those elephant fights for which Lucknow has been long celebrated … a female elephant, followed by two horsemen well mounted and armed with long spears, was conducted into the enclosure …'[7] Two male elephants

William Daniell
Elephants fighting at Lucknow
Engraving
Private collection
© Look and Learn, Elgar Collection / The Bridgeman Art Library

Richard Earlom
after Johan Zoffany
Tiger hunting in the East Indies, 1802
Mezzotint
21⅛ × 26¾ inches · 538 × 680 mm
© The Trustees of the British Museum

were then introduced, with the idea that they would be induced to fight for the female. Zoffany has shown the moment of engagement between the two male elephants, surmounted by Mahouts, the horseman carrying their long spears, are in the process of encouraging the fight. The elephant on the left of the composition has been backed into the river Gompti, confirming the location of Zoffany's scene as Asaf-ud-daula's palace complex at Gow Gautee. Zoffany has captured the drama of the scene, using the white chalk to represent clouds of dust and the churned water of the Gompti, and the rearing horses, running figures and small dog to suggest the scale and energy of the engagement. Beyond the fight, Zoffany has included Gow Gautee itself, showing an arcade, terrace and awning. Under the awning several figures are visible, including a seated man, dressed in European costume – wearing a tricorn hat and leaning on a stick – and seated on what appears to be a dais to the far right, a figure that is likely to be Asaf-ud-daula himself. Described with remarkable economy, in a few rapid lines of chalk, these characteristic details are entirely legible to the viewer, underlining Zoffany's extraordinary ability as a draughtsman.

Zoffany's highly energised composition is the most spectacular and engaging of his surviving Indian drawings. Characteristic in approach – rapidly drawn in chalks – this newly discovered sheet demonstrates a greater ambition in content than the other surviving sheets. Not a topographical view, like most of the few surviving drawings from this period, it displays the drama and scope of a historical work and should perhaps be read in the same mode as *Colonel*

Morduant's Cock Match. Zoffany retained the drawing in his studio until his death and there is evidence that he used it once back in Britain to help create an Indian composition: *The Tiger Hunt at Chandenagore, Death of a Royal Tyger* (Victoria Memorial Hall Calcutta) of 1790–95. Zoffany transposed the two figures in the foreground of the present drawing directly into the foreground of the *Tiger Hunt*. This remarkable sheet of *Elephants Fighting* therefore remained an important memorial of Zoffany's time in India and particularly in Lucknow amongst the cultivated friends he made there, but also a resource from which he could draw once he was established back in London.

We are grateful to Charles Greig and Dr Martin Postle for their help with this catalogue entry.

NOTES

1   Ed. Martin Postle, *Johan Zoffany RA: Society Observed*, Exh. Cat., New Haven (Yale Center for British Art), 2012, p.38.

2   Mary Webster, *Johan Zoffany*, New Haven and London, 2011, p.483.

3   Mary Webster, *Johan Zoffany*, New Haven and London, 2011, p.644.

4   Mary Webster, *Johan Zoffany*, New Haven and London, 2011, p.492.

5   Mary Webster, *Johan Zoffany*, New Haven and London, 2011, p.490.

6   M. Hardie and M. Clayton, 'Thomas and William Daniell: their life and work', *Walker's Quarterly*, 35 and 36, London, 1932, p.65. For Daniell's sketch see: Maurice Shellim, *Additional oil paintings of India and the East by Thomas Daniell RA and William Daniell RA*, London, 1988, p.13.

7   William Daniell and Hobart Caunter, *The Orienatal Annual, or Scenes in India*, London, 1835, II, p.131.

Johan Zoffany
A Dying Hindu brought to the River Ganges, 1788
Black, red and white chalk · 10⅝ × 13⅝ inches · 270 × 346 mm
Yale Center for British Art, Paul Mellon Collection, New Haven

JOHAN ZOFFANY 1733–1810

Portrait of an unknown man

Oil on canvas laid down on panel,
6 × 4½ inches · 152 × 115 mm, oval
Painted in the 1770s

COLLECTIONS
Robert Gallon (1845–1925);
Private Collection, UK.

This highly engaging, previously unpublished portrait by Johan Zoffany represents an important addition to his *oeuvre*. Exceptionally finely painted, the portrait study is unfinished and thus provides us with some information about Zoffany's working method. Zoffany's wide ranging training and career encompassing Germany, England, Grand Tour Italy and India has recently received much scholarly attention: a biography appeared in 2009 followed by a comprehensive survey of his works by Mary Webster in 2011, the same year in which a major exhibition of over a hundred of his works was held at the Yale Center for British Art and Royal Academy of Arts in London.[1] This attention has prompted a reassessment of Zoffany's role as one of the most versatile and acute observers of British society, but also as one of the finest portraitists of the eighteenth century.

The identity of the sitter of the present portrait has, thus far, proved elusive. Given the immediacy, confidence and most importantly scale of the likeness, it seems likely to be a study for one of Zoffany's conversation pieces rather than a full-size portrait. Stylistically it probably dates from the 1770s, the decade Zoffany was at the height of his powers, when he executed several of his most enduring compositions including *Portraits of the Academicians of the Royal Academy* and *Tribuna of the Uffizi*. In preparation for the first of these monumental canvases, commissioned by King

George III to commemorate the foundation of the Royal Academy of Arts in London, Zoffany made a series of small-scale oil studies, at least one of which survives.[2] In February 1772 Zoffany went to Bath to paint Thomas Gainsborough for inclusion in the conversation piece, the resulting portrait study remained with the sitter's family until it was presented to the National Gallery in 1896 and subsequently transferred to the Tate in 1955.[3] Like the present picture, the portrait of Gainsborough is fluidly painted and left unfinished, the sitter is seen animatedly looking to the right and would have served as a model for inserting the head into the finished conversation piece. Along with Gainsborough – who seems likely to have refused inclusion on the grounds of his growing animosity towards the hanging committee – the brothers George and Nathanial Dance were also omitted from the group. Sadly the history of our work gives us no clue as to the identity of the sitter, the painting is first recorded in the collection of the nineteenth-century landscape painter Robert Gallon who does not seem to have any obvious connection to a known Zoffany sitter or patron. The quality of the present work makes its anonymity particularly tantalising.

For Zoffany friendship was frequently expressed through portraiture and the intimate scale and unfinished nature of the present work reinforces the idea that it was the study of someone he knew well. We know Zoffany was in the habit of painting oil studies during theatrical performances, a fact confirmed by the rare survival of two studies of *David Garrick as Abel Drugger in The Alchymist* at the Ashmolean, and this head may be the result of studying one of

Johan Zoffany
Thomas Gainsborough, c.1772
Oil on canvas
7¾ × 6¾ inches · 197 × 171 mm
© Tate, London 2013

his friends from the theatre. The partially painted canvas reveals Zoffany's characteristic off-white ground, which is visible at the bottom of the canvas, beneath the sitter's white stock.[4] Fluid lines of light brown paint are also clearly visible and these are characteristic of Zoffany's method for blocking in the features and poses of his sitters. The head itself is bought up to an extraordinarily high level of finish, the features are handled with characteristic delicacy, adding unblended passages of highlight to impart a vitality to the expression. The portrait, which was cut-down at some point and laid-down on a mahogany panel, survives in outstanding condition and directly demonstrates the vivacity and incisiveness with which Zoffany drew with the brush.

We are grateful to Dr Martin Postle for confirming the attribution of the painting to Zoffany.

NOTES

1 Penelope Treadwell, *Johan Zoffany: Artist and Adventurer*, London, 2009; Mary Webster, *Johan Zoffany*, New Haven and London, 2011 and ed. Martin Postle, *Johan Zoffany RA Society Observed*, exh.cat. New Haven (Yale Center for British Art), 2012.

2 Mary Webster, *Johan Zoffany*, New Haven and London, 2011, pp.261–260.

3 ed. Martin Postle, *Johan Zoffany RA Society Observed*, exh.cat. New Haven (Yale Center for British Art), 2012, cat.no.45.

4 For an analysis of Zoffany's working method see: Jessica David, 'Zoffany's Painting Technique: *The Drummond Family* in focus', in ed. Martin Postle, *Johan Zoffany RA Society Observed*, exh.cat. New Haven (Yale Center for British Art), 2012, pp.167–174.

LOWELL LIBSON LTD
BRITISH ART

Lowell Libson Ltd specialises in British art with an emphasis on paintings, watercolours, drawings and sculpture of the seventeenth to mid-nineteenth centuries. We count many leading North American, European and British museums and private collectors amongst our clients.

Lowell Libson has over thirty-five years experience in dealing. Formerly he was a director of Leger Galleries and Managing Director of Spink-Leger Pictures. He is a member of the organising committee of *Master Drawings & Sculpture London,* a member of the executive committee of the *Society of London Art Dealers* and the *Walpole Society* and in 2011 was appointed a member of the *Reviewing Committee on the Export of Works of Art and Objects of Cultural Interest.* The gallery's research is led by Jonny Yarker who recently completed a PhD at the University of Cambridge and has a considerable reputation as a scholar of British painting and the Grand Tour. He has published widely

and held academic fellowships in America, London, and most recently, Rome. Day to day management of the gallery is in the hands of Deborah Greenhalgh who has long and valuable experience in the art market.

Lowell Libson Ltd actively supports art historical research in Britain and America. The gallery has mounted a number of important loan exhibitions including *Masterpieces of English Watercolours & Drawings* from the National Gallery of Scotland and works by Thomas Rowlandson drawn from British private collections. Lowell Libson Ltd. have sponsored a number of exhibitions including: *Thomas Gainsborough's Landscapes* at the Holburne Museum, Bath, 2011; *Constable Gainsborough Turner and the Making of Landscape* at the Royal Academy, 2012. In 2014 we are sponsoring the Wright of Derby exhibition at the Holburne Museum and are supporting *A Dialogue with Nature* at the Morgan Library, New York.

We believe that the process of acquiring a work of art should be an enjoyable and stimulating experience and have created a gallery that offers clients the opportunity to discuss and view pictures in discreet and comfortable surroundings. We act as both principals and agents in the purchase and sale of works of art giving clients great flexibility and choice. We offer advice on all aspects of collecting pictures. This includes the purchase and sale of works of art as well as conservation, restoration, framing, lighting and hanging. The gallery also provides a complete curatorial service for collections. Visitors are always welcome at the gallery, which operates on a 'by appointment' basis, to view pictures or to discuss their collections.

3 Clifford Street · London W1S 2LF
Telephone: +44 (0)20 7734 8686
Email: pictures@lowell-libson.com
Website: www.lowell-libson.com